HOKIES

HANDBOOK ™

Stories, Stats and Stuff
About Virginia Tech™ Football

By Chris Colston
Foreword by Frank Beamer

Printed in the United States of America by
Mennonite Press, Inc.

ISBN 1-880652-65-X

PHOTO CREDITS All photographs were supplied
by the Virginia Tech Sports Information
Deptartment, Dave Knachel and Kacy
Jahanbini.

Doug.
May the Orange Bowl
not be the high watermark
for the Hokies - Enjoy.

ACKNOWLEDGMENTS

Vinny.
Christmas
1996

Think back to some of your golden memories of Virginia Tech. It's October. The sun is shining but there's a briskness in the air. Sweater weather. The leaves are a brilliant mixture of gold, brown, red — and Chicago Maroon and burnt orange. Old friends mingle before the game.

For more than a century, Virginia Tech football games have served as a rallying point for the university, a gathering together for one common goal: to cheer the Hokies to victory. Through the years there have been many great reasons to cheer. This book gives fans a chance to revel in the history of Virginia Tech football.

As with any book of this type it could never have been finished without the help of many people.

Thanks to Bill Dooley, who along with Jack Williams gave me the chance to show what I could do with the Hokie Huddler back in 1985.

Virginia Tech's Sports Information staff was invaluable throughout the writing process. Special thanks to Williams and Dave Smith for their input, advice and ideas; Anne Panella for taking the time to e-mail me all those statistics; and Dave Knachel for his fine photography and letting me rummage through his files.

Thanks to former Tech SID Wendy Weisend for his contributions on Tech football during the '60s and '70s.

Thanks to all the players throughout the years for their candid and often wry observations.

Thanks to Bill Roth for your contributions to the book as well as overall ideas and feedback.

Special thanks to Roland Lazenby. Your fine work in *Legends* has become required text for any true Hokie fan and was a great source for most of the early material in this book.

Thanks also to *The Roanoke Times*; Drew Kubovcik for his patience in helping out whenever the need arose; my brother, Steve Colston, for his suggestions and/or hibba-like comments and observations; John Hunt for his general friendship and creative ideas; Kacy Jahanbini for his photographs; and Damian Salas for his work on the bowl statistics.

Thanks to head coach Frank Beamer, who authored the foreword. I was there for both your lean times and glory years, and I can think of no more deserving man to earn success than you. Thanks for creating so many great memories for all of us Hokie fans out there.

For my parents, Jim and Jo, who without their support and encouragement this book would never have been written.

C.C.

FOREWORD

Football always has been special in our town. There's something really magical about a Saturday at Lane Stadium/Worsham Field.

The sport at Virginia Tech has produced so many great teams and so many legendary players. Who will ever forget Carroll Dale, the silky-smooth receiver of the 1960s who went on to help win three National Football League championships with the Green Bay Packers? Then the 1980s produced one of football's all-time greats in Bruce Smith, who sacked everyone in sight and won the Outland Trophy.

This book recounts the feats of those guys and salutes the great teams — from the powerhouse squad of 1932 to the unbeaten team of 1954 and to the 1986 team that won the Peach Bowl on a last-second kick by a player named Chris Kinzer.

It is my opinion, however, that the face of Virginia Tech football is changing. We are right in the middle of it. It is dramatic and sweeping.

It was my privilege to be a part of one of the best teams ever in 1995 when Tech won 10 games in a row and swept the championships of the Big East Conference and Sugar Bowl. The stirring win over Texas in the Superdome turned Bourbon Street into a Hokie celebration none of us will ever forget.

With three straight bowl trips and Tech's membership in the prestigious Big East, Tech suddenly has changed from a state team, one that attracts attention across the commonwealth, to a team of true national stature.

I do not take credit for the change. I was just lucky to be at the right place at the right time. The change was inevitable because of the popularity and the vitality of the sport in our community and because of fans who are just as special as the men who play the games.

The best is yet to come. There is no doubt in my mind that Tech will soar to more unprecedented heights. We are reaching for the stars. Nothing less will satisfy any of us. Virginia Tech will be among the best teams in college football on a year-to-year basis.

One thing, however, will not change. The spirit surrounding the sport in Blacksburg will forever be magical.

I'm proud to be coach of the Hokies and a part of the Virginia Tech family. Thanks to all those who love Tech football for affording me the honor of coaching your team.

It's fun and it's magical!

— *Frank Beamer, 1996*

TABLE OF CONTENTS

1892-1950
The Early Years

Football at Virginia Tech started in the early 1890s, when the game was more like a cross between boxing and rugby. Professor Ellison A. Smyth — who headed Tech's biology department for 34 years and has a campus building named after him — had played football at Princeton and wanted to start the sport in Blacksburg.

According to Roland Lazenby's book, *Legends*, college President Dr. John McBryde thought the rigorous exercise of this new sport would "eliminate mischief from the minds of students." So he went with the idea.

'YOU'RE ON YOUR OWN, BOYS' Although McBryde supported the idea, that was the extent of his succor. The college provided no funding and the players purchased their own equipment, including a Walter Camp football purchased via mail order for $1.25.

COME OUT AND PLAY Tech's first team captain was professor W.E. Anderson, who played right tackle. Professor Ellison Smyth acted as trainer and business manager. Cadets H.B. Pratt and J.W. Stull helped him organize the squad. But being on the team didn't have the glamour or notoriety that it holds today; often players

This early team was a motley-looking bunch.

had to go into the barracks and plead with cadets to give up some free time to come out just to hold practice.

GO LONG AND HEAD FOR THE TRACTOR Games were pretty much a disorganized mass of confusion. "There was no idea of team play," wrote Virginia Agricultural and Mechanical College's college yearbook, *The Bugle*. "Whoever got the ball — by luck — ran with it. The boundaries of the field were marked off with a plough."

Tech's first playing field ran up and down a hill, according to the Bugle, "with interesting little hollows which hid the play from spectators on the other side."

1. Who was Virginia Tech's first paid coach?

FIRST GAME It wasn't until that next fall that the university fielded its first football squad. The first game came on Friday, Oct. 21, 1892, in Blacksburg versus St. Albans, a private boys preparatory school in Radford. Professor Anderson scored the first touchdown in Tech history as the boys from Blacksburg prevailed, 14-10.

WHERE THERE'S A WILL Coaches today complain Blacksburg is "hard to get to." Flying commercially requires a stopover and then a 45-minute bus ride from Roanoke. But that's nothing compared to St. Albans' trip that day: The schoolboys traveled in three horse-drawn surries and crossed the New River on a ferry. According to *Legends*, "a hat was passed on the sidelines to collect admission from the members of the corps who had come out to see this newfangled entertainment."

'WE WANNA GET EVEN' In classic competitive style, St. Albans wanted to get even and requested a rematch in Radford the following weekend. St. Albans took a 10-0 lead as the teams talked trash to each other. The arguing got so vehement that captains from both teams decided to stop play, giving the game to St. Albans. Tech finished its first season 1-1.

2. What Hokie great lost his right hand in an accident when he was 13 but went on to become athletic director at Alabama?

IMAGINE THAT — IT'S FLAT After a couple of struggling seasons, J.A. Massie took over as coach. For the first time, football players were allowed to arrive on campus early after summer vacation. Upon returning, they found a field that was — get this — actually flat. President McBryde donated part of the agricultural gardens, a stony bean field located in part of the area that is now the famous Drillfield.

Those grounds were called Scheib Field, named after E.E. Sheib, who helped organize Tech's first athletic association. Later it was called Gibboney Field in honor of James Gibboney, the school's first graduate athletic business manager. In 1908, the name changed to Miles

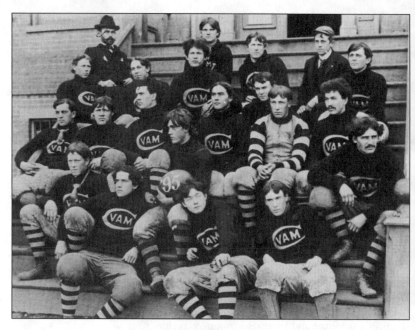

It wasn't actually "C-VAM." It was VAMC.

field, for Sally Miles. When Tech built a new, $101,000 field in 1926, it was named Miles Stadium. It was the Home of the Hokies for 40 years.

VAMC We're referring to the university as Tech, but before 1896 there was no such thing. The school was known as VAMC, and no, that didn't stand for Virginia Motor Company. It stood for Virginia Agricultural and Mechanical College, and the "Vamcies" wore black and cadet gray — colors that today would be considered "cool."

SHORT AND SWEET — AND OBSOLETE Not so cool, however, was the school's first sports yell:

> "Rip, Rah, Ree!
> Va, Va, Vee!
> Virginia, Virginia!
> AMC!"

COLORS ONLY A HOKIE COULD LOVE In 1896 Tech changed its name to Virginia Polytechnic Institute and its colors to Chicago maroon and burnt orange. The colors were chosen by a committee because they made a "unique combination not worn elsewhere at the time." Or any other time. Tech wore the colors in a game for the first time on Oct. 20, 1896.

SO WHAT'S A HOKIE? Tech needed a new cheer and offered a prize for the best offering. O.M. Stull, Class of 1896, won the contest by composing the now famous words:

> *"Hoki, Hoki, Hoki, Hy!*
> *Tech! Tech! VPI!*
> *Sola-Rex Solah-Rah*
> *Polytech-Vir-gin-i-a!*
> *Rae, ri VPI!"*

3. What are "Lesters?"

And there's the answer for fans, media and everyone else who ever wondered what the heck a "Hokie" was — a figment of Stull's vivid imagination. He admitted the word had no meaning. "I thought it sounded good," he said.

One question: if he invented the nickname, how come he misspelled it?

AND WHAT'S UP WITH 'GOBBLERS?' One story says that "Gobblers" came from HOW Tech football players ate — not WHAT they ate — as observed by the school's good-natured cadets. Hmm. A nickname based on voracious appetites? Well, that's their story and they're sticking to it.

FIRST MASCOT In *Legends*, Roland Lazenby tells a great story about Tech's first mascot, a lively African American by the name of Floyd "Hard Times" Meade. For games he dressed as a clown and performed as a kind of one-man band. He understandably grew tired of the clown schtick, however, and began feeding and training what he billed as "The Largest Turkey in Montgomery County."

By the first game of the 1912 season, his new act was

Floyd "Hard Times" Meade

ready. He hitched his bird to a small cart and rode around the field — single-handedly promoting both of Tech's nicknames, Gobblers and Hokies.

The act was such a hit that Meade would train a turkey to pull his cart around the field for the annual Thanksgiving Day game. He rewarded the bird's efforts by having him for dinner.

Hunter Carpenter was the greatest Tech player of the early years — and one of the all-time greats.

THE REIGN OF CARPENTER Current Virginia Tech sports information director Dave Smith has been with the Hokies so long, those in the athletic department joke that he was roommates with Hunter Carpenter, who arrived on campus in 1898 as a 15-year-old freshman.

Had Smith been around then, he might have seen Tech's greatest-ever football player.

"Carpenter was a back in the class of Jim Thorpe and Red Grange," wrote Douglas McKay, a member of South Carolina's 1905 squad.

HE'S A HOKIE. NO, A TAR HEEL. WAIT … According to *Legends*, the athletic associations of the day had no firm eligibility rules. So Carpenter — who in five seasons never played on a Tech team that beat his most hated rival, Virginia — decided to pursue graduate studies at North Carolina. The 1904 Tar Heels had a strong team and had a better chance of beating the Cavaliers. It didn't matter. Virginia beat UNC, 12-11, before a record crowd of 15,000.

Carpenter turned down an offer to be Carolina's 1905 captain and instead returned to Tech as a graduate student.

Hunter Carpenter behind center during a Hokie practice. Recognize any of the campus buildings?

HE WAS NO PRO Like so many die-hard Hokies, Carpenter was obsessed with beating the Cavaliers, and the 1905 team was good enough to do it. He led Tech to a 16-6 upset of Army on Oct. 14. The Hokies also notched an 86-0 win over Roanoke College (Sept. 30) and waxed Carolina, 35-6, on Oct. 28. But all season

Carpenter was pointing to the UVa game scheduled for Nov. 4. A few days before that game Wahoo officials accused Tech of paying Carpenter, making him a professional, and called off the affair. Tech denied the charges, but the Wahoos said they wouldn't play if Carpenter did.

NOW THIS IS A RIVALRY According to *Legends*, Virginia finally called off the game two days before it was to be played. Carpenter and the Hokies said they were coming anyway. Only after day-of negotiations between Tech and Virginia officials was the game a go.

Carpenter scored two touchdowns to give Tech an 11-0 lead. The hotly-contested game was marked by voluminous profanity and dirty play, with players taking swings and punches at each other.

C.P. "SALLY" MILES — MR. VPI

When C.P. Miles enrolled at Tech in 1897, he had no idea he would stay for 60 years. Over the years he performed virtually every athletic job possible, from player to conference president. He was often referred to as "Mr. VPI."

Miles was baseball coach in 1912. From 1920-35 he was athletic director and helped form the Southern Conference in 1921. He then served as VPI's dean from 1943-51.

As great a contributor as he was to Tech, Miles had the dubious distinction of being in power for two moves that would haunt the Hokies to this day. He was Southern Conference president when 13 of the 23 members broke away to form the Southeastern Conference in 1932, and he was Tech's faculty chairman when seven more schools left to form the Atlantic Coast Conference in 1953.

Miles wanted to keep athletics in perspective and wanted to steer clear of conflicts with academics. In 1932, for instance, the Hokies

C.P. Miles

were ranked No. 11 in the nation. Although the ranking was short-lived, it still could have worked for Tech, according to *Legends*. Prior to the Alabama game, a group of Memphis entrepreneurs invited the Hokies to play in a bowl game against Mississippi. But "Mr. VPI" was opposed to postseason games. He was president of the Southern Conference at the time and lobbied to have Tech officials turn down the invitation.

Imagine that happening in the 1990s.

Miles died in May 1965, just months after Tech had demolished Miles Stadium and had pulled out of the Southern Conference — the league he helped form.

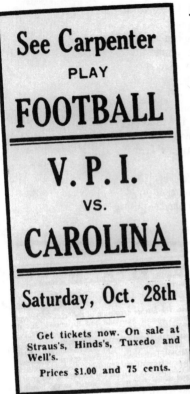

See Carpenter

PLAY

FOOTBALL

V. P. I.

VS.

CAROLINA

Saturday, Oct. 28th

Get tickets now. On sale at Straus's, Hinds's, Tuxedo and Well's.

Prices $1.00 and 75 cents.

Hunter Carpenter was quite an attraction in his day, as this promotional flier attested.

Tech had 45 shutouts in 78 games from 1900-09.

The Hokies' starting 11 in 1909 averaged 172 pounds.

JUST A-SWINGIN' One Virginian had slugged Carpenter several times early in the game. When Carpenter broke loose on a long run, the same fellow tracked him down, grabbed him by the neck and took another swing. Carpenter stopped, decked his antagonist, winged the ball into the crowd and left the field. Talk about grand exits.

MISSION ACCOMPLISHED — SORT OF The Hokies held on to win the game, 11-0, and Carpenter had finally beaten the Cavaliers. But because of the controversy the two teams would not play again for 17 years. Instead Tech played William & Mary twice the following season.

Carpenter might have felt some guilt about the discontinuation of the series, but he maintained his innocence. "My father [a well-to-do Clifton Forge businessman] paid all my college expenses," he told his nephew, Deverton Carpenter, a Richmond newspaper reporter. "If I had received any help, he would have made me quit playing football the moment he heard of it. The charges were completely untrue."

Even though Carpenter played seven years of college, remember that he never played in high school and was just 22 when he finished his collegiate career. He led the Hokies to a 9-1 mark in 1905, his last season. Carpenter is a member of the National Football Hall of Fame.

WE'RE THE GREATEST From 1894 to 1919, Tech had 26 straight seasons without a losing mark. After going 4-6 in 1920, the team then rolled off 10 more winning campaigns.

Tech publicist Mel Jeffries apparently got caught up in the excitement when he wrote:

"Yes, the sculptors of Ancient Greece chiseled out the marble to athletes who couldn't compare to the greatest of Tech gridmen, in ability or finesse."

IT'S ABOUT TIME Tech's first complete pass didn't come until four years after starting the sport — in 1906, against William & Mary in Blacksburg. It was a real bomb, too. Fullback Russell Smith threw two yards to Herbert David Hodgson in a 28-0 win.

Varsity Eleven & Substitutes

The first scoring pass came in 1907, also against Washington & Lee. Quarterback Cleveland Edward Sheppard to P.P. Huffard. In classic style, the pass was intended for H.H. Varner, but Sheppard overthrew him.

BRANCHING OUT Branch Bocock became Tech's first paid coach in 1909. He came to Tech from the University of Georgia and led the Hokies to one of its best seasons ever.

The Ivy League is anything but big-time football today, but in the early 1900s it was *the* league, and Princeton was a national power. The Tigers handed Tech its only loss in 1909, kicking the winning field goal on the game's last play for an 8-6 final. Tech finished with a 6-1 record and declared its players "Champions of the South." Never mind that Virginia finished 7-1 and lost to northern-power-at-the-time Lehigh. The two teams didn't meet on the field, so each could lay claim to being "The Best."

FIRST ASSISTANT COACH Bocock went 34-14-2 in six seasons but left after the 1910 season for North Carolina. He returned in 1912, and athletics had grown so much that in 1915 the university deemed it necessary to hire an assistant coach for Bocock. It hired David Munsick of Cornell to serve as line coach.

PEAKE PERFORMANCE Tech sports publicist H.H. "Bunker" Hill deemed the backfield of Frank Woodfin Peake (a 6-foot, 170-pound back), Scotty McArthur, Tommy Tomko and H.M. "Mac" McEver the "Pony Express."

Peake was the star bronco in the Express. "He was perfectly proportioned, lithe and slender and was exceedingly durable," wrote Tech publicist Mel Jeffries. "Hard tackling that would be punishing to many ball

Early VPI players — such as these "Tecks" from 1901 — were compared to chiseled Greek statues. Hopefully they moved a bit quicker.

Tech went 59-22-5 from 1910-1919.

Frank's career Peaked in Blacksburg.

H.M. McEVER — COACH MAC

Although Frank Peake was the star of the "Pony Express" backfield, H.M. "Mac" McEver became the more well-known — and maybe the best-loved — Hokie in school history.

McEver played from 1925-29, then helped coach Tech teams in football, basketball and baseball. In addition to playing sports year-round, he served as class president. He served as Tech's head football coach in 1945 and shared head duties with Tex Tilson in '42. He returned to Tech in 1951 as executive secretary of the Tech Student Aid Association. A member of the Tech Hall of Fame, McEver retired in 1979.

Whenever someone asked McEver what was the greatest moment in Tech athletics, he would reply, "It hasn't happened yet." But he finally saw it — Tech's 1995 Sugar Bowl victory over

H.M. "Mac" McEver

Texas — three weeks before his death.

A Hokie fan once asked McEver what his initials stood for. "The H stands for H-ornery," he said, slightly changing the pronunciation of the word. After scratching his head for a good number of seconds, the fan finally said, "But ornery doesn't start with an H."

McEver smiled and told him it actually stood for Herbert, but that he hated the name. The M stood for Macauley, "but it's almost impossible to say Macauley and McEver in the same breath." So H.M. — or "Mac" — it was.

Mac McEver does his best Red Grange imitation.

carriers held no terrors for Frank Peake. Tacklers very rarely got a solid 'shot' at him. He was seldom hit a solid blow, nor did he fall hard. When running he was as fleet and graceful as a gazelle. Peake would wear only a lightly padded leather helmet, light weight shoulder pads, almost no hip pads, thigh pads or knee pads. 'More than that just slows me down and bothers me,' he insisted."

Joe Moran was a star center on Tech's 1925 and '26 teams.

SARTORIAL SPLENDOR Black and white photos give that old-time feel when reflecting about the old days of football. It's almost hard to imagine that the uniforms actually had color in them. Until the early 1930s, Tech's standard uniform consisted of maroon jerseys and khaki pants. In 1931, coach Orville "Slippery" Neal changed all that. It must have been a sight to see the Tech players in orange jerseys and helmets with maroon stripes and bright maroon pants.

Neal, constantly irritated by the pain from an old war wound in his foot that never healed, missed several games as Tech notched its first losing record (3-4-2) in a decade. He then married a coed and left campus.

Former Tech star Henry "Puss" Redd replaced him. Two other former Hokie greats, William "Monk" Younger and Sumner D. "Tex" Tilson, joined him on the staff.

If playing talent made a good assistant coach, then Redd hired the right guys. The legendary Walter Camp dubbed Younger "The Southern Panther" after witnessing a stellar defensive performance in a 19-0 loss to undefeated Yale. Tilson was a hard-blocking lineman.

Sumner "Tex" Tilson

1932: REACHING NEW HEIGHTS

Going into that fresh season, there was an air of de-emphasizing athletics. Maybe Tech was just trying to rationalize the losing season; who knows. But winning games became less important to the powers that be. "The real aim of our football and all our athletics is the development of physical fitness and moral character in our students," VPI President Dr. Julian Burrus said. "If we fall short of this greater aim, we fail. If we achieve it, we win, and the score of the game makes only minor difference."

With such a rousing motivational speech, Redd's boys went out and had a great 1932 season anyway. The team didn't have any superstars, "just a bunch of smart boys who knew how to play football," according to McEver, who was the freshman coach.

Captain Bill Grinus was VPI's top defensive player. Charlie Morgan played quarterback and Al Casey was the runner deluxe, a man who could do 50 one-armed pushups. The Hokies even had a one-eyed end, Al

Captain Bill Grinus was an anchor for the '32 Techies.

Hank Crisp overcame a handicap to have a stellar athletic career.

Tech (in light jerseys) battled mighty Alabama in Tuscaloosa before losing, 9-6. There's no truth to the rumor that the players had lemonade in the house in the background afterward.

Seamon. The team took only 24 players on the road, and just 18 saw much action.

HEADED FOR GLORY After a 32-7 romp over Roanoke College on Sept. 24, 1932, the Hokies beat Georgia, 7-6, on Oct. 1 after Grinus broke through the line and blocked an extra point late in the game.

But the greatest win of the season came two weeks later as undefeated Kentucky came to town. The largest crowd in Miles Stadium history, estimated at between 8,000-10,000, witnessed a 7-0 Tech win. Then, after a 32-6 win over Washington & Lee, the Hokies were ranked No. 11 in the nation and were headed to face Alabama for the Southern Conference championship. Bama's athletic director was former Tech star Hank Crisp, who lost his right hand in an accident when he was 13.

NO. 3 IN THE SOUTH Led by Red English and Bill Porterfield, VPI's great defense did a superb job containing Crimson Tide All-American running back Johnny "Hurry" Cain. The two stopped Cain four times inside the Tech 4-yard line in the third quarter, and Tech led 6-0 going into the final period.

Alabama, using a platoon system, finally began to wear down the short-handed Hokies in the fourth and went on to win, 9-6. Even so, the players were treated like heroes when they returned to Blacksburg. Tech finished the season 8-1 and was the third-ranked team in the South, behind Alabama and Tennessee.

A MISPLACED ACE Basketball star Adrian Custis might not

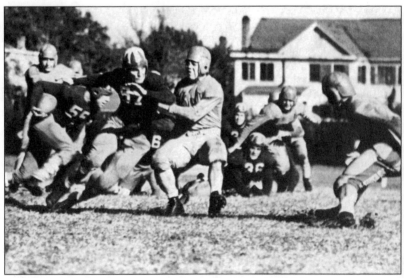

have been Tech's first "Ace" if the school had shown a little more moxie following the '32 season. Clarence "Ace" Parker, a hot prospect out of Portsmouth, was being courted by schools all over the country, in particular by Duke and its recruiter Eddie Cameron. The Hokies had an "in," however: Assistant coach Dick Esleeck, a Portsmouth native, knew Parker.

And he knew Parker was lacking an English credit. In what would have been a blatant recruiting violation today — but was perfectly legal then — McEver and Esleeck brought Parker to Blacksburg for the summer, tutored him in English and gave him a job playing for a local semi-pro baseball team.

Everything clicked marvelously, and just before the start of fall practice, Parker wanted to take a weekend trip

Henry "Puss" Redd guided one of the greatest teams in school history.

COULD TECH HAVE BEEN IN THE SEC?

Virginia Tech's rousing 1932 season put it in place to move up in the growing world of college football. Instead, it took a giant step backward.

"Across the region, sportswriters were talking about the up-and-coming bunch from Blacksburg," Lazenby wrote in *Legends*.

"But within days after the close of the season, the world of southern football changed. The large schools of the South — Alabama, Georgia, Auburn, Tennessee, Kentucky — were headed for the big time of college athletics. Like Notre Dame, Army and Navy, they wanted to win. The athletic directors were eager to raise money from their alumni, and they wanted to broadcast games over the radio. But the Southern Conference officials, led by Tech's Sally Miles, insisted on keeping a ban on fund-raising. Faced with that opposition and their own desire to grow, the South's large universities elected to withdraw from the Southern and form the Southeastern Conference."

North Carolina, Clemson,

Duke, N.C. State, South Carolina, Maryland, VMI and Washington & Lee remained behind.

"It left the Hokies in a position of not really striving for athletic excellence," Lazenby wrote. "Although Tech coaches did little recruiting, the school still offered 13 or 14 athletic work-scholarships a year, funded from profits the Athletic Association made from the campus bookstore. Other schools were offering twice that number by raising money from alumni. Mac McEver, then the freshman coach, felt certain that even in the heart of the Depression he could raise $5,000 from alumni for another dozen scholarships. Redd and Sally Miles would have none of it. 'Puss never believed in fund-raising,' McEver said of Redd. 'Alumni never gave money the whole time he coached. We made ourselves mediocre in the old Southern Conference. We got so far behind we never caught up.' "

"It all went back to the decision to de-emphasize athletics," Red English said.

home. Tech figured everything was cool, so the coaches gave him his English certificate and put him on a train.

Cameron, whose contacts keep him informed of Parker's whereabouts, learned of the trip and boarded the same train. By the time they had arrived in Portsmouth, Cameron had convinced Parker to sign with Duke.

With Parker doing it all — running, throwing and kicking — the Blue Devils won 24 of their next 29 games. Parker went on to a Hall of Fame career in the NFL.

If only Tech had waited to give Parker his English certificate until he returned for practice … .

MEDIOCRITY After missing so many opportunities, it's no wonder Tech began to stumble. It went 18-16-5 from 1933-36, then fell to 3-5-2 in 1938 and 4-5-1 to close out the decade.

Basketball star Adrian Custis nearly wasn't Tech's first "Ace."

A TRUE HERO H.J. "Herb" Thomas was Tech's scoring leader at the turn of the decade. But he will go down as one of the university's all-time greats for something he did on the battle field, not the playing field. A Marine sergeant in the Pacific during World War II, Thomas was leading a group of nine men against a Japanese pillbox on Bougainville Island when a hand grenade dropped into their foxhole. Thomas threw himself on the live grenade, saving the lives of his men. He was awarded the Medal of Honor posthumously. He also won the Navy Cross. A community hospital in South Charleston, W.Va., was named after him, as were a dormitory on Tech's campus and a USS destroyer built in 1945. His portrait hangs in the Third Marine Headquarters in Hawaii.

TOUGH TIMES Because of World War II, Tech did not field

HOKIES QUIZ

4. If All-American center Jim Pyne was going to have a cologne, what did he jokingly say it would have to be called?

Herb Thomas won the U.S. Medal of Honor for bravery.

TURKEY DAY TRADITION

It's only appropriate that for the longest time the highlight of any Gobbler football season came on Thanksgiving Day. That's when VPI met VMI in Roanoke for "The Military Classic of the South."

Roanoke's Chamber of Commerce could only drool over the downtown atmosphere created by the event. Streets and storefronts were dressed with joyful Christmas decorations. Downtown hotel lobbies were filled with revelers as orchestras played and ballrooms rocked.

"What the game used to be was an almost breathless socio-economic event which often seemed to have very little to do with football," *Roanoke Times* columnist Ben Beagle wrote in 1968. "It was the kind of game which sold fur coats to women for the occasion. And for Roanokers and other western Virginians, it was a curious but successful mixture of old home week, Mardi Gras and Christmas five weeks early … It was a game of flasks and chasers in the rumble seat; all the girls were beautiful, all the fans loyal and Army-Navy wasn't a bit better."

As Tech grew and VMI remained a small military school, the event began to lose its allure. Tech officials ended the Thanksgiving day game in 1970.

VPI-VMI on Thanksgiving Day was a big social event. This game-day parade in downtown Roanoke, circa 1930s, started the festivities.

After the war, Mac McEver had to rebuild Tech's football program.

teams in 1943 and '44. McEver basically had to start the program from scratch again in 1945, and the team limped to a 2-6 record. But one of the wins came against one of the greatest coaching legends in college football history, Paul "Bear" Bryant, then head coach at Maryland.

THE BLACKBOARD SIX According to *Legends*, the Hokies practiced against a defense called "the Blackboard Six." The only problem was, very few teams played that defense.

Nobody used the defense, that is, but Maryland. Figuring the Terrapins would beat the Terra-ble Techsters, Bryant instead focused on the next opponent. The fired-up Hokies, salivating at the sight of "the Blackboard Six," pulled a 21-13 upset.

THE SUN BOWL Under coach Jimmy Kitts, Tech finished 3-3-3 in 1946, including a 49-0 loss to William & Mary, a Southern power at the time. The Hokies obviously didn't possess earth-shattering talent, but it didn't matter: An alumnus who was a big official with the power company in El Paso had a hand in selecting teams for the Sun Bowl.

Despite the efforts of star tackle John "The Greek" Maskas, Tech fell to Cincinnati, 18-6. The Sun Bowl paid the Hokies $8,500 for their participation.

YOU GET WHAT YOU PAY FOR Tech's lack of commitment to football caught up to it in a big way in the late 1940s. Other area schools were catching on that it took money to build a successful program. But Redd and Younger, the athletic director, maintained Tech needed no more money. In 1948, under the restricted budget and new coach R.C. McNeish, the Hokies played five games before scoring. They finished 0-8-1.

WE'RE MAD AS HELL AND WE'RE NOT GOING TO TAKE IT ANYMORE Tech probably felt like things couldn't get any worse after it finished 1-7-2 in 1949. Ha, ha. The 1950 squad went 0-10 and was outscored 430-66, an average of 43-6 per game. The Hokies set a national record for most kickoffs received. Undoubtedly, those Hokies were the worst team in school history.

Fed up, a group of alumni began raising money without the consent of Redd or Younger.

Head coach Jimmy Kitts led Tech to the 1946 Sun Bowl.

Tech became the first team from the Commonwealth of Virginia to play in a postseason bowl — the 1946 Sun.

1951-1970
Rough & Tough

In 1951, it was time to hire a tough, hard-nosed coach to pull up the Tech program up by its bootstraps. Enter Frank O'Rear Moseley, 39, who left Bear Bryant's staff at Kentucky to come to Blacksburg. According to *Legends*, Tech President Dr. Walter S. Newman offered him the longest and most lucrative contract ever for a Tech coach, a whopping $10,000 annually for five years. He would also serve as athletic director.

Of the 26 scholarship football players in the class of 1953, only three finished their playing eligibility.

THE WAR In a student aid association newsletter, Moseley wrote that only about 21 of the 50 players on scholarship "had any possibilities at all." The rest were not worthy, and Moseley's intense, demanding practice sessions ran off the weak.

"It was like we were in a war," center/linebacker Jack Prater told *The Hokie Huddler* in 1986, "and we were the survivors."

WHY, YES, WE ARE Prater shared a story that put things in perspective. It also explained perhaps why the 1954 Tech team — the only undefeated squad in school

FRANKLY SPEAKING

The Virginia Tech Student Aid Foundation, formed in 1949, raised about $10,000 and the group was eager to make a presentation. So several members gathered for a meeting at a Roanoke hotel with Frank Moseley.

"If that's all you've got," Moseley was quoted in *Legends*, "just keep it."

Lazenby's book also says that Moseley shocked the crowd into giving another $9,000 that evening.

Moseley, one of six charter members to the Tech Hall of Fame, served as athletic director from 1951-78.

"Somehow Tech's new leader in inter-collegiate athletics carries about him the air of a man who would do well in a battle with the devil himself," stated the Jan. 15, 1951, *Techgram*.

An apt description of the man known as "Mose."

No-nonsense Frank Moseley took over as head coach and athletic director in 1951.

history at 8-0-1 — was so successful.

"Our season opener was against the North Carolina State Wolfpack, who ran the single-wing offense," he said. "Lenoir-Rhyne College also ran the single-wing, so one day that August we drove down to scrimmage them.

"While one of our platoons scrimmaged, the other two ran wind sprints, like always. After the practice the Lenoir-Rhyne players came up to us and said, 'That was some kind of punishment, right? What did you guys do?' We just looked at them. 'You mean you guys don't do that?' we asked. They said, 'No, are you *crazy*?' "

Jack Prater, a member of Frank Moseley's earlier teams and later a Tech fund-raiser, likened those first practice sessions to war.

1954: A GOLDEN TEAM

Moseley's greatest team was the '54 squad that rose as high as No. 9 in the Associated Press national rankings and finished the year at No. 16.

In 1988, *The Hokie Huddler* readers voted this squad the greatest in school history.

Decked out in long-sleeve maroon jerseys with shiny orange sewn-on numerals, white facemask-less helmets with one maroon stripe, and white pants, the Hokies weren't big. But what the team lacked in size — nobody weighed more than 220 pounds — it made up for in speed and savvy. It had great senior leadership in ends Tom Petty and Bob Luttrell, guards Billy Kerfoot and Jim Haren, quarterback John Dean, halfbacks Howie Wright and Billy Anderson and tackle George Preas.

That team finished 8-0-1, the tie coming against William & Mary when the Indians' Doug Henley intercepted a Billy Cranwell pass and returned it 55 yards for a score.

PREAS & NUTTER Center Madison "Buzz" Nutter, the first Tech player ever drafted by the National Football League, played 12 years with the Baltimore Colts. He was drafted by the Washington Redskins but was cut after six games, perhaps because he was too tall (6-foot-4) for 5-foot-2 quarterback Eddie LeBaron to see over him. "Eddie had to reach UP to get the snap from me," Nutter said when he was inducted into the Tech Sports Hall of Fame in 1985.

Buzz Nutter, a Tech Hall of Famer, was the first Hokie to be drafted by the NFL.

When Baltimore picked him up, the Colts had two Hokies on the offensive line who were good enough to help win the 1958 and '59 NFL championships. Preas spent 11 years on the Colt offensive line, and he and Nutter protected one of the greatest quarterbacks in NFL history, Johnny Unitas.

Preas started 40 straight games for the Hokies. Moseley called him "the greatest lineman I ever coached."

In 1956, Tech finished the year as the No. 2 rushing offense in the nation with 2,835 yards, just behind Oklahoma.

LEFT OUT Virginia Tech had no idea at the time, but a 1953 development left the Hokies in a football hole it would not emerge from until joining the Big East. That's when North Carolina, Wake Forest, Duke, North Carolina State, South Carolina and Maryland left the Southern Conference to form the Atlantic Coast Conference.

After those disastrous campaigns of the late 1940s, Tech's reputation hit rock bottom. That's probably why Tech wasn't asked to join despite heavy campaigning on Moseley's part. Yet the league took UVa in 1954. By the time Moseley had made the Hokies desirable, the ACC wasn't looking to expand. The Golden Year of 1954 came a few seasons too late.

RETRIBUTION FOR THE QB Tech continued to win under Moseley, going 6-3-1 in 1955. One of the season highlights came against William & Mary, a school the Hokies had not beaten in 17 years. Down 7-0 at intermission, Tech scored two unanswered touchdowns in the second half for a 14-7 victory. It was an especially sweet win for Billy Cranwell, whose interception

Quarterback Billy Cranwell, left, atoned for an earlier miscue.

accounted for the Indians' only touchdown in the previous season's tie. He threw a 71-yard touchdown pass to Dave Ebert.

A SHIFT IN MOSE'S PRIORITIES The Hokies went 7-2-1 in 1956, rising to as high as No. 16 in the nation. The 1957 team was supposed to be one of Moseley's best; he was

ALL HAIL DALE

The highlight of Tech football in the late 1950s was a rangy, glue-fingered, hard-blocking end named Carroll Dale.

In 1958, Dale was named Southern Conference Player of the Year and was a second-team Associated Press All-America selection. A year later, as a senior, he made three first-team All-America squads: Football Writers, *LOOK*, and the Newspaper Enterprises Association. Dale became Tech's first football All-

American and was invited to play in the Blue-Gray and Senior Bowl games.

The Los Angeles Rams drafted him in 1960 and he caught a touchdown pass in his first professional game. After five years the Rams traded him to Green Bay, where he started on three straight championship teams under Vince Lombardi. He was named to the NFL Pro Bowl in 1970 and '71.

Dale is a charter member of the Tech Hall of Fame.

The September, 7, 1957, edition of the Saturday Evening Post named Tech receiver Carroll Dale as the top sophomore lineman in the nation, making coach Frank Moseley, left, a happy man.

In 1958, Billy Holsclaw, nephew of former Tech star Duncan Holsclaw (1932-34), became Tech's first 1,000-yard passer.

so confident, in fact, that he moved his office upstairs to concentrate on administration. After beating Tulane, 14-13, in New Orleans — it was Tech's first-ever win over a Southeastern Conference team — the team struggled and finished 4-6. The '58 team got back in the winning column by finishing 5-4-1.

The Hokies had a strong 6-4 mark to close out the decade. Moseley's last Tech team was his 1960 squad that went 6-4. According to *Legends* a 9-7 loss to Davidson convinced Moseley to let someone else do the coaching while he concentrated on his duties as athletic director. He had dreams of a new stadium and still believed he could convince the ACC to add Tech.

ENTER JERRY CLAIBORNE Moseley kept the Bear Bryant legacy going by hiring Bryant assistant Jerry Claiborne. Moseley was an assistant coach at Kentucky when Claiborne was a player.

Jerry Claiborne

Claiborne was named the Wildcats' Most Valuable Senior in 1949. He became an assistant under Bryant at Kentucky in 1952, then followed Bryant to Texas A&M and became the Aggies' defensive coach. That 1956 squad ranked No. 8 nationally in total defense.

Claiborne's reputation as a defensive genius grew at Missouri, where he devised a pass defense that ranked second in the nation. He rejoined Bryant at Alabama and helped the Crimson Tide lead the nation in pass defense in both 1958 and '59.

He was the type of man who had the letters KISS framed on his office wall: Keep It Simple, Stupid.

He had the qualifications. Now he had the chance to build a program.

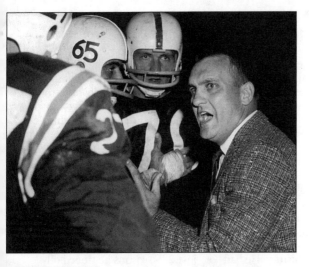

Under Claiborne, Tech added "UCLA" stripes around the shoulders of its jerseys for the first time ever.

GREATNESS DELAYED Keeping Moseley assistants Bill Conde, Dick Redding and Jack Prater helped ease the transition, but Tech still finished 4-5 in 1961, its first year under Claiborne. Things would heat up the following year. The season of 1962 marked quarterback Bob Schweickert's debut. One of the most exciting players in Tech history, Schweickert unfortunately suffered a shoulder injury and missed most of the Hokies' first six games. But he came on strong upon his return, with a 74-yard run against Tulane and a 96-yard quarterback sneak against Wake Forest en route to a 5-5 campaign.

Coach Jerry Claiborne and some selected players admire their 1963 Southern Conference Championship banner.

SOUTHERN CONFERENCE CHAMPIONS Schweickert and fullback Sonny Utz formed Tech's famed "Mr. Inside and

MR. OUTSIDE

Bob Schweickert had a maniacal work ethic. He didn't walk to classes, he ran; to improve his accuracy, he would throw 300 to 400 passes a day. The hard work paid off; in 1963, he completed 62 of 116 passes for 687 yards and ran for another 839, averaging 5.4 yards per carry. His 1,526 yards of total offense set a Southern Conference record.

What a versatile athlete he was. Schweickert once returned a punt 82 yards against VMI, the second-longest in Hokie history. He had six 100-yard rushing games and stands eighth on Tech's career passing list. He ranks 13th on Tech's career rushing list — amazing for a quarterback.

And talk about closing strong. He did not toss an interception in his last eight games as a senior. When he wasn't running or passing, he was booming punts, averaging 37.8 yards in his career. He rose to the occasion in a 1964 win over Floirda State, with punts of 51, 58 and 65 yards.

But the thing most people remember about Schweickert were his long, dazzling runs. In just 2 1/2 seasons he ripped off touchdown scampers of 74, 96, 63, 59, 59 and 66 yards. His 96-yarder remains a school record.

No. 10, Bob Schweickert, was a dangerous man in the open field.

Mr. Outside" duo. Between them they accounted for almost 70 percent of Tech's offense from 1963-64.

The two were never better than the 1963 game against Richmond on Nov. 2. Schweickert rushed for a then-school record 204 yards on 29 carries, while Utz added 132 yards in a 14-13 Tech victory. Tech won its only outright Southern Conference championship that season.

THE GAME MADE HIM HURL The Hokies notched one of their all-time great wins in 1964, beating No. 10 Florida State, 20-11. Seminole receiver Fred Biletnikoff was so frustrated by the day's proceedings that, after scoring a fourth-quarter touchdown, he hurled the football out of Miles Stadium.

Tech's next game was its last ever in Miles, and the Hokies made it memorable with a 27-20 win over

Frank Moseley stands proudly in front of the press box of the new Lane Stadium.

MR. INSIDE

Silas Alex "Sonny" Utz, a rough-and-tumble fullback under Coach Jerry Claiborne, was one of Tech's true wild and crazy characters. "Sonny lived in the fast lane," said Tommy Walker, Utz's junior year roommate who went on to become an Army pilot. "Coach had a practice of rooming the mellow players with guys who were rough around the edges.

"One night I was trying to convince Sonny that we both had big tests the next day. He wasn't in the mood to study. Some guys were out in the hallway playing around and they started a water battle. I pleaded with Sonny to come back to the room, and he commenced to take a trash can, fill it with water and dump it over my head."

One night, Utz and some teammates had been partying and "we decided to go out to a nearby pasture to mess around," teammate Vic Kreider said. "The cows out there started charging us. Sonny put a couple of them down with a tackle."

Sonny Utz was a rough-and-tumble fullback who enjoyed life.

Lean Gene Breen, left, was one of four Hokies to be named All-Southern Conference.

Bob Schweickert, right, graced the cover of Tech's 1964 Gridiron Guide.

In 1963, for the first time in school history, the Hokies had four players named to the Southern Conference first team: Schweickert, Utz, Gene Breen and Newt Green.

William & Mary.

Tech moved into Lane Stadium for the 1965 season, playing its first game on Oct. 2 — a 22-14 win over Virginia. Dickie Longerbeam rushed 28 times for 164 yards to take Star of the Game honors. Lane Stadium was still under construction and would not be officially completed until 1968.

FEELING INDEPENDENT In 1964-65 Tech announced it was leaving the Southern Conference and compete as an independent. President T. Marshall Hahn said Tech wanted to schedule schools with larger athletic programs, but secretly he held hopes that the school would be admitted into the ACC.

SIGH — A TIE It seems whenever Tech and West Virginia meet in football, the sky is gray, there's a mist in the air, and the defenses rule. Low-scoring, hard-hitting, and ugly: That's the way to describe Hokie-Mountaineer football games.

That was never truer than on Oct. 1, 1966, when Tech and WVU played in a downpour at Lane Stadium in Blacksburg.

Tech dominated the game statistically, with 74 offensive plays to WVU's 37 and 305 total offensive yards to West Virginia's 109.

But with three minutes left in the game West Virginia led, 13-7.

Tech rallied, and Ken Barefoot's 1-yard run in the final minutes tied it at 13. But placekicker Jon Utin

GREAT WARRIOR, TRAGIC LOSS

Even though he was only 5-foot-9 and 175 pounds, defensive back Frank Loria became Tech's first consensus All-American and earned the same honor the next season. A devastating hitter, Loria had seven career interceptions and returned 61 punts for 813 yards and four touchdowns. Tech went a combined 22-7-1 during his tenure.

Despite his stellar career, no NFL team drafted him. Loria did some graduate work at West Virginia University then joined the coaching staff at Marshall under Rick Tolley, a Tech linebacker from 1959-60. On Nov. 14, 1970, the team's Southern Airways DC-9 crashed just short of the Huntington airport runway. Loria and Tolley were among the 75 fatalities in the tragic accident.

Loria was one of six original members inducted into the Virginia Tech Hall of Fame. His jersey No. 10 has been retired.

Frank Loria was Tech's first consensus All-American.

missed the extra point. The game finished a tie, the only deadlock in the series that dates back to 1912.

SPRINGBOARD TO A BOWL Tech was 4-1-1 in that '66 season when Florida State came to town on Oct. 29. The largest crowd ever to see a football game in the state — 31,000 — was on hand for the game, televised regionally by ABC and a rookie announcer by the name of Keith Jackson. Tech won, 23-21, with the difference being a Dan Mooney tackle in the end zone for a first-quarter safety. Frank Loria had an 80-yard punt return for a score.

It was the key win in an 8-1-1 regular season that earned Tech a bid to the Liberty Bowl against Miami.

"Hang On Sloopy" by the McCoys was the nation's No. 1 song when Tech played its first game in Lane Stadium.

THE '66 LIBERTY BOWL Virginia Tech traveled to Memphis for the Dec. 10 bowl, its second postseason trip ever. Miami won, 14-7, but Tech took some pride in finishing the season ranked No. 20 by United Press International.

Jimmy Richards'
blocked punt set up
Tech's only score in
the '66 Liberty Bowl.

A blocked punt by Jimmy Richards in the first quarter led to Tech's only touchdown of the game. Miami's defense held the Hokies to just 111 yards of total offense.

Tech's defense was tough as well, holding the Hurricanes to 163 yards, including 55 on the ground. A roughing-the-kicker penalty in the third period led to Miami's first score, and Hurricane quarterback Bill Miller directed a fourth-quarter drive that ended in Miami scoring on fourth-and-goal from the 1-yard line.

Frank Beamer, who
as head coach would
later would lead the
Hokies to their
greatest heights ever,
was part of some
glory years as a
player, too.

RISE — THEN THE FALL Tech won its first seven games of the 1967 season and rose to No. 19 in the United Press International poll. Interest was high as the Hokies faced their Liberty Bowl foe, Miami, for homecoming in front of a record crowd of 35,000. There was no revenge, however, as the Hurricanes won, 14-7. The next week the Hokies fell to Florida State, 35-14, then were upset by VMI, 12-10.

REVENGE WAS THEIRS VMI was fired up because a year earlier, in a 70-12 loss, Claiborne had reinserted running back Tommy Francisco in the lineup to score his sixth touchdown of the game. Instead of heading to a second straight bowl game, Tech stayed home.

"To this day I can remember how great we felt when we were ranked and how empty we felt after losing our last three and not going to a bowl," Frank Beamer said in 1993.

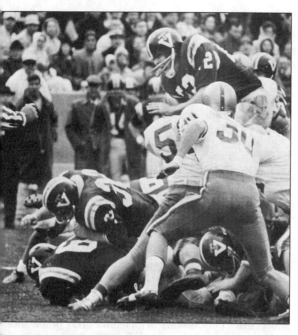

Tommy Francisco's 1966 touchdown romp served to fire up VMI the following year.

SO, WHAT DID THE *CRITICS* SAY? Prospects weren't altogether bright for 1968. Even Tech's own *Gridiron Guide*, put out by its sports information office, was pessimistic. "In a nutshell: [Tech has a] lack of experience and depth, especially in the interior offensive and defensive lines, a shade slower in team speed than in 1967, an unproven passing attack, so far a dearth of veteran leadership — and the toughest schedule in the history of the school."

Frank Beamer lowers the boom on an opposing receiver.

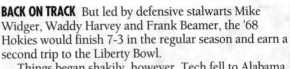

From 1963-67, Tech was the 12th winningest major college football program in the country (36-13-1).

BACK ON TRACK But led by defensive stalwarts Mike Widger, Waddy Harvey and Frank Beamer, the '68 Hokies would finish 7-3 in the regular season and earn a second trip to the Liberty Bowl.

Things began shakily, however. Tech fell to Alabama, 14-7, at Birmingham with Larry Creekmore (who later was a Tech assistant coach) blocking a punt and Jud Brownell falling on it in the end zone for Tech's only score.

After a 2-3 start, the Hokies were struggling offensively. Starting quarterback Al Kincaid had missed time with injuries, but he returned. Claiborne also moved Ken Edwards to running back. The move juiced Tech's attack. In the team's final five games — all wins — Edwards and tailback Terry Smoot banged out 1,080 between them. Included in the streak was a 40-22 waxing of No. 18 Florida State on Nov. 2. The Seminoles were a 14-point favorite.

He wasn't big, but linebacker Mike Widger got huge results.

HE FELT LIKE AN ALL-AMERICAN Widger became one of the season's biggest surprises. He wasn't big — 6-foot, 190 pounds — but he played like a giant. An unknown going into the season, he earned Associated Press first team All-America honors with an incredible array of statistics.

He had seven interceptions for 203 yards and earned 825 tackling points, which according to the 1969 media guide was akin to "landing on the moon."

Sports Illustrated named him its national Lineman of the Week for his performance against South Carolina on Nov. 16, when he had 15 tackles, 14 assists, four sacks and an interception in Tech's 17-6 win.

THE 1968 LIBERTY BOWL Coming off a record-setting 55-6 win over VMI on Nov. 28 to close out the regular season, the Hokie offense didn't miss a beat in the first quarter of the Liberty Bowl against Mississippi. Tech set a Liberty Bowl record with 17 first-quarter points.

But that would be it. Behind quarterback Archie Manning, Ole Miss stormed back for a 34-17 victory. Steve Hindman bolted off tackle for a 79-yard score on the first play of the second half to put Mississippi ahead for good.

FALL OF THE CLAIBORNE ERA The Hokies would not earn a bowl bid for another 12 years, and the 1969 season was a down one as Tech dropped to 4-5-1. The Hokies lost their first five games of 1970, and President T. Marshall Hahn called Claiborne into his office. Hahn, already irked by Claiborne's earlier comments that it was difficult to recruit top athletes to Virginia Tech, told him the current season would be his last.

"Tech president T. Marshall Hahn Jr. took an active

role in the Claiborne firing," wrote *Roanoke Times* sports editor Bill Brill. "Hahn would like too see Tech as a football power every year.

"Under Claiborne, the Hokies had their moments of glory and played in two Liberty Bowls. But the last two teams had losing records, the freshmen teams were sub-par, and Tech was out-recruited in the state for the first time since Claiborne arrived.

"Alumni contributions to athletics at Tech had not dropped off in total money, but the number of contributors had. While Claiborne still retained a staunch group of followers, their number decreased."

The Hokies then won five of their final six games under Claiborne. The loss, a 34-8 setback to Florida State, came on the same day Loria died in the plane crash — Nov. 14, 1970, one of the blackest days in Tech football history.

A GREAT ONE Claiborne's career wasn't finished by any means. He went on to Maryland where he coached from 1972-81, then directed Kentucky's program from 1982-89. His 179 career wins makes him tied for 26th on the all-time NCAA list.

In early 1969, coach Jerry Claiborne signed Tech's first black football player, John Dobbins, a running back from nearby Radford.

Frank Loria, a two-time All-American at Tech, died in a plane crash while on the staff at Marshall.

1971-1977
Strugglin' '70s

The 1970s were not the best of times for Virginia Tech. The Hokies would not go to a single bowl in the decade, they would put together just two winning seasons, and they combined to win just 47 games in the 10 seasons. Tech went through four coaches — Jerry Claiborne, Charlie Coffey, Jimmy Sharpe and Bill Dooley — and as many uniform changes. It was a time of turmoil for the program, but there were bright spots.

TECH'S COFFEY BREAK Instead of the "Little Alabama" attitude Tech had maintained under Moseley and

New Tech coach Charlie Coffey, right, allowed mop-haired quarterback Don Strock to do his thing.

Coffey intended to build a "Fence of Pride" around the state of Virginia.

Claiborne (both Bear Bryant disciples), new head coach Charlie Coffey tried to make Tech a "Little Tennessee." A Volunteer himself, Coffey did away with the maroon and gave Tech burnt orange jerseys and white helmets. Even the athletic offices were painted bright orange.

In 1971, tight end Mike Burnop — the analyst on Tech's football radio network — caught a school-record 46 passes.

"The state of Virginia is our backyard," Coffey proclaimed, "and we intend to build a 'Fence of Pride' around it."

To emphasize the point, Coffey put an orange state of Virginia on the sides of Tech's new white helmets, with "TECH" stenciled across it in bold maroon letters.

STROCK TALENT UNLOCKED Coffey came to Blacksburg as a defensive coach; he was the defensive coordinator at Arkansas under Frank Broyles from 1966-70. But he would make his mark at Tech on the opposite side of the ball. The beneficiary was quarterback Don Strock.

Freed of Claiborne's run-oriented attack, Strock flourished under Coffey's pass-happy philosophy. Instead of emphasizing defense, Coffey hired Florida State offensive coordinator Dan Henning to liven the Hokie attack.

Although Tech went just 4-7 in 1971, Strock — a rising junior — completed 195 of 356 passes for 2,577 yards, the second-highest total in the nation. The coaching change might not have been the best move in Tech history, but it saved Strock's career.

THE GOBBLIN' SCOREBOARD One of the great pleasures of attending games in the 1960s and '70s was Lane Stadium's

5. A large VT graces the side of a grassy hill along Southgate Drive just off Rt. 460 on the Virginia Tech campus. It is composed of 210 neatly-trimmed bushes. What kind of bushes are they?

Don Strock runs here, but he was better known for his arm at Tech.

scoreboard, which featured a wild, gobbling, blinking, flashing beanie-capped Fighting Gobbler. Bill Dooley took it down when he arrived at 1978, but sometimes, when the sun is setting on a tailgate and the ice is melting in the bourbon-and-Coke, alumni get misty-eyed thinking of that old crazy thing.

OOH, OOH, SEVENTY-TWO Don Strock was just getting warmed up in '71. The following year he burned up the Hokie record books.

Against Houston that year, Strock passed for 301 yards in the first half alone as Tech took a 20-7 lead. He finished the day 34 for 53 for 527 yards — all three Hokie records.

But Tech lost three fumbles — two inside the Houston 5-yard line — and the game ended in a 27-27 tie.

WILD WIN The Hokies had another wild one in Lane Stadium a few weeks later against 19th-ranked Oklahoma State. Tech trailed, 32-31, with less than a minute to play. Don Strock fumbled close to the goal line, but Tech recovered. With 12 seconds left, his brother, Dave, attempted a field goal but missed to the right. Officials called the Cowboys offside, and Strock converted the 18-yarder for a 34-32 win.

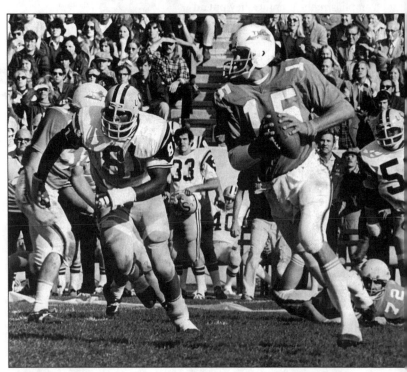

STROCK SHOCK Tech finished 6-4-1 in '72 as Don Strock passed for 3,170 yards, the fourth-highest total in NCAA history. His 427 attempts and 228 completions that season still stood as Tech records in 1996, as did his per-game average of 294.8 yards passing.

With his great year, Strock captured the national passing title — and the hearts of Hokie fans everywhere.

Miami picked Strock in the fifth round of the NFL Draft, and he had a long career with the Dolphins.

GOING BACKWARD AGAIN Coffey and the Hokies must have had post-Strock Syndrome in 1973, as they lost their first six games. The happiness of a 27-15 win over Virginia — if you're gonna break a losing streak, that's the team you want to do it against — was short-lived, however.

THE ALL-TIME WAXING The following week Alabama crushed the Hokies, 77-6 — the worst loss in school history. The Crimson Tide — which finished the regular season ranked No. 1 — piled up 833 total yards, 748 of them on the ground. Bama's 11.9 yards per carry set an NCAA record and four players ran for more than 100 yards.

Michael Jackson's "Ben" topped the charts the week Tech upset No. 19 Oklahoma State on Oct. 14, 1972. Other hits of the week included "Everybody Plays The Fool" by the Main Ingredient and "Go All The Way" by the Raspberries.

Wide receiver Ricky Scales stands second on Tech's all-time pass receiving list with 113 receptions. His 2,272 career receiving yards are a school record.

Bear Bryant recommended Jimmy Sharpe to Virginia Tech.

The gap between Tech and college football's upper echelon never seemed so vast. Moseley, Tech's athletic director and a close friend of Bear Bryant, was never in favor of hiring Coffey, and some wondered if Bryant was trying to make Coffey look bad. If so, he succeeded. Tech finished a woeful 2-9, and Coffey was fired.

'MOSE' LOOKED SHARPE Moseley, still athletic director, was never happy with Coffey as head coach. He figured it was school President T. Marshall Hahn's hire. So when it came time to find a replacement, Moseley went back to the well that quenched his thirst before: Bryant. The Bear's recommendation: a former guard on Alabama's 1961 national championship team, 34-year-old Jimmy Sharpe.

'DADGUMMIT' Gone were the orange jerseys and back were the maroon, with white numerals trimmed in orange. And once again Tech was starting over, this time with a Wishbone offense. Among his assistants were Charley Pell, who eventually took over at Florida, and Danny Ford, who won a national title at Clemson in 1981.

Rick Razzano loved Tech's bare-belly jerseys.

In an early press release, Sharpe said he would make only two promises. "We will work," he said, "and we will hit."

Sharpe was a homespun type who was fond of saying

"Dadgummit" on his weekly television show.

During a 1976 game, Sharpe actually wore a sweat-shirt with ironed-on letters on his back that said, "I'm A Hokie And Proud Of It." Remember, this was the '70s.

HOKIES QUIZ

RAZZANO A DYNAMO One of Sharpe's greatest players was a stocky linebacker who was about as wide as he was tall. Nobody recruited Rick Razzano of New Castle, Pa., who wasn't big (5-foot-11, 205 pounds) and wasn't very fast either.

Pitt, Penn State, Purdue and Indiana all turned him down. The New Castle coaches loaded Razzano, John Latina and Nick Rapone in a van and brought them south in search of scholarships. And Tech needed players.

Sharpe didn't realize what a stud he had. Razzano went on to record a Tech-record 368 tackles. He even played professionally with the Cincinnati Bengals.

Razzano and high school teammates Latina and Rapone had "a great time at Tech," he said. "Every August we'd shave our heads and grow Fu Manchu mustaches, and during the season we'd wear those ol' half-jerseys that showed your belly button."

6. Tech's nine-game winning streak heading into the 1996 season is the longest in school history, breaking the record of eight set in what season?

HE SCORED! NO, WAIT … Tech lost its first four games of 1974 and finished 4-7. One of the most heartbreaking defeats of that year was a 28-27 setback to Virginia in Charlottesville on Oct. 19. Both teams had entered the contest with 1-4 marks.

UVa's Scott Gardner threw a pair of fourth-quarter touchdowns to give the Cavaliers a 28-14 lead.

Phil Rogers went from running back to quarterback for Tech.

At the age of 30, Arians became the youngest head coach in NCAA history when Temple hired him in 1983.

Things looked bleak for the Hokies, who were running the Wishbone offense — not the greatest comeback attack in college football. But quarterback Bruce Arians completed a 24-yard pass to Rickey Scales, setting up a 1-yard touchdown sneak by Arians with 7:44 left. The pass play was Tech's first completion in nine quarters.

On the last play of the game, Arians and Scales hooked up again on an 11-yard touchdown pass. Virginia argued, to no avail, that Scales had one foot out of bounds. Sharpe could've sent out his placekicker and taken the easy tie, but ...

"We decided to go for the win and try a two-point conversion," Arians told *The Hokie Huddler* in 1986. "I ran an option to the right, and halfback George Heath threw a great block to spring me. I landed waist-high in the end zone, and then I heard all this screaming.

"All of our guys were yelling that we won the game. By now I'm at the bottom of a big pile, then I hear UVa start to scream that *they* had won the game. I'm still lying under there with the ball in the end zone, but one of the officials ruled no score.

"The linesman was supposed to make the call, but he was nowhere to be seen. The other referees didn't say anything, and they just ran off the field."

In the book *Hoos 'N Hokies, The Rivalry,* Arians told Doug Doughty that he knew one of the officials, Brian McDevitt, from high school. "He always tells me, 'We knew you scored, but Scales was out of the end zone.' "

The St. Louis Cardinals drafted Phil Rogers in the fifth round of the NFL Draft. He went on to a career in the Canadian Football League.

1975: SURPRISING SUCCESS

Sharpe's led the Hokies to an 8-3 mark for his best season at the helm. Rogers, Beasley, Razzano, tailback Roscoe Coles, defensive back Billy Hardee, defensive lineman Mike Faulkner, offensive tackle Rondal Davis and linebacker Doug Thacker were the team's stars. Tech might have gone bowling that year but was just 4-3 at

Roscoe Coles stands second on Tech's all-time rushing list with 3,459 yards. He led the Hokies in rushing three straight years (1975-77).

Wayne Latimer holds the record for the longest field goal in Tech history: 61 yards.

one point. The Hokies won their last four games, but by the time people realized how good they were the bowl bids were taken.

One of the biggest wins of '75 came Oct. 4 at Auburn, with the Hokies prevailing, 23-16. The defense put up a late goal-line stand, and Coles had an 89-yard touchdown run. "We're a team now," Sharpe proclaimed after the victory.

The Hokies also beat Florida State. It seemed like whenever Tech had a big win in a big season, it came against the Seminoles. The Hokies won, 13-10, in '75 after Wayne Latimer kicked a school-record 61-yard field goal.

Another great win that season came on a brilliant sunny Oct. 18 afternoon in Lane Stadium, when the Hokies beat Virginia, 24-17. The game helped to atone for the previous year's heartbreak. The game was still in doubt, however, until Beasley sacked Cavalier quarterback Scott Gardner late in the game. Gardner fumbled and Mike Stollings recovered with less than a minute left.

BLOCKING BEASLEY WASN'T EASY As a senior, Beasley was an All-South Independent selection and an honorable

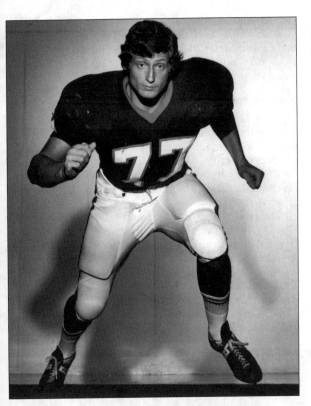

Tom Beasley had the big sack in '75 against Virginia.

mention All-America pick. The Pittsburgh Steelers drafted him in the third round and he had a 10-year professional career, earning two Super Bowl Championship rings. Tech inducted him into its Hall of Fame in 1988.

'CHOKIES?' Hopes were high going into 1976. The bowl bid that never was a year earlier was expected to come this season, and bumper stickers proclaimed Tech was "Bowl-Bound In '76."

And it looked that way for awhile. Tech won six of its first eight games, including victories over rivals Virginia (14-10) and West Virginia (24-7).

Then the bottom fell out. Tech blew a game at home to Tulsa, 35-31, on Nov. 6. After leading by 10, Tech allowed two fourth-quarter touchdowns. The Hokies still could've pulled the game out when they recovered a fumble with two minutes to go at the Tulsa 18-yard line and got a first down. But with second-and-six and less than a minute to play, they lost a fumble.

Tech also fumbled a punt that Tulsa got on the 5 and muffed a punt attempt that Tulsa got on the 3-yard line. The term "Chokies" was heard more than once around

When Tech beat Virginia in mid-October of 1975, "Miracles" by Jefferson Starship and "Born To Run" by Bruce Springsteen were receiving heavy radio air play.

campus that night.

After that setback the Hokies lost to Richmond (16-0) and Florida State (28-21) to finish a disappointing 6-5. FSU pulled out two fourth-quarter touchdowns for its victory.

A SEASON TO FORGET The Hokies struggled to a 3-7-1 mark in '77. Tragedy struck the program before the last game of the season when freshman fullback Bob Vorhies died in his dormitory room from cardiac arrhythmia. A member of Tech's coaching staff had put Vorhies through punishment drills because he violated a team rule, and the player's family filed a lawsuit. The case was settled out of court.

The Hokies fired Sharpe after the disastrous season. Once again they were looking for a new coach — and now an athletic director. At age 66, Moseley decided it was time he retired.

Big No. 88, Mickey Fitzgerald, was a devastating running back — when given the chance.

THE INCREDIBLE HULK One of the few bright spots of 1977 was the play of Mickey Fitzgerald, "The Incredible Hulk." On Nov. 5 Sharpe switched him from tight end to a Wishbone fullback against No. 15 Florida State. He

pounded out 112 yards on 25 carries as the Hokies almost upset FSU before falling, 23-21. The next week he carried 28 times for 144 yards against West Virginia. The Hulk was loose! Against Wake Forest he had 30 carries for 142 yards and scored three touchdowns, marking the first time in school history that a running back had gained more than 100 yards in his first three starts. In the final game of the '77 season, he gained 104 yards and scored three more touchdowns. He was just getting started, yet there were no more games.

Unfortunately, Fitzgerald's glorious run would be short-lived. When Sharpe resigned, Tech hired a man who believed a fullback was a blocker first, a runner second.

HOKIES QUIZ

7. What is the highest Virginia Tech has ever been ranked in football?

1978-1986
The Dooley Years

8. What is the highest the Hokies have ever been ranked by the Associated Press?

Moseley. Claiborne. Coffey. Sharpe. All were hot-shot assistants who were given chances to build a program by Virginia Tech. In 1978, the Hokies wanted to hire a proven commodity. University President William Lavery found just that in North Carolina head coach Bill Dooley by offering him the dual role of coach and athletic director.

Dooley had been to six bowls in the last eight years and had raided the state of Virginia for many of his top recruits, including linebacker Lawrence Taylor, who went on to become one of the greatest players in NFL history. The Hokies had rounded up a bonafide winner.

"DOO-LEY! DOO-LEY! DOO-LEY!" chanted Tech students when Lavery introduced the new Hokie coach during a Tech basketball game.

It was a back-to-basics hire. Dooley, a conservative coach in the mold of Moseley and Claiborne, got rid of the "frivolous" orange trim on Tech's outfits and went with plain maroon jerseys. Tech went back to maroon helmets, not worn since 1970. A single bold maroon stripe adorned the white pants.

He even took the "Beanie-Hatted Gobbler" off the scoreboard and replaced him with a bland, generic-looking maroon "Fighting Gobbler" logo.

When the Hokies hired Bill Dooley, they got a man who wasn't afraid to get down and dirty.

"PURPLE 98" Dooley's first season was forgettable (4-7) save for a wild 22-19 win over William & Mary on Sept. 30, 1978.

Trailing 19-15, Tech had the ball at midfield with time for one play. Quarterback David Lamie dropped back and heaved a 50-yard bomb to wideout Ron Zollicoffer. Surrounded by three defenders, Zollicoffer came down with the ball, juggling it as he fell to the ground. The ball popped loose, but officials ruled he had possession long enough, and Tech pulled out a miracle 22-19 win.

Exile's "Kiss You All Over" was No. 1 the week Tech beat William & Mary on a last-second Hail Mary pass. "Boogie Oogie Oogie" by A Taste Of Honey was No. 2.

Ron Zollicoffer had possession of this ball long enough to register a touchdown.

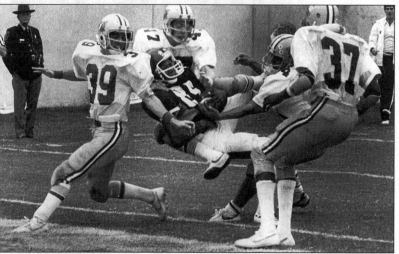

"The play was called 'Purple 98,'" Lamie said. "The receivers do various cuts and wind up in the same area. When I came to the line and was calling the signals, I noticed the free safety was standing at his 5-yard line. I dropped back about six or eight yards and just threw it."

AN 'I' PROPONENT One of Dooley's trademarks was a grind-it-out, ball-control I-Formation offense featuring a strong-running tailback. The man who fit the bill in 1978 was Kenny Lewis, who rushed for 1,020 yards and 10 touchdowns. A year earlier, he had carried just 33 times for 160 yards.

Although the spotlight had shifted away from him, fullback Mickey Fitzgerald had another strong season with 545 yards and was a devastating blocker.

Under Bill Dooley, Kenny Lewis came out of nowhere to become a 1,000-yard rusher.

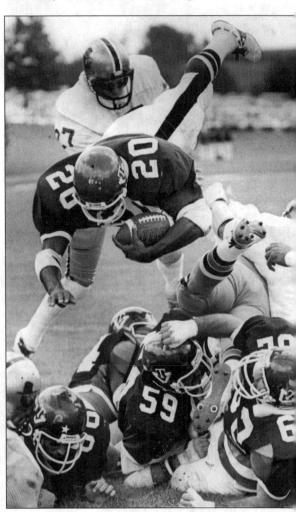

PASSING THE TORCH? The following season, 1979, stocky Cyrus Lawrence joined Lewis in the backfield. Lawrence rushed for 791 yards, Lewis 748, as Tech went 5-6. That would be Dooley's last losing season in Blacksburg. Unfortunately, longtime Tech Athletic Director Frank Moseley would not live to see it. He died in July of 1979, less than two years after his retirement.

HOKIES QUIZ

9. How many ranked teams did the Hokies beat in the 1995 Sugar Bowl Championship season?

GIG 'EM? In the summer of 1979, Virginia Tech's sports information department ran a contest asking fans for a new Hokie slogan. Among the entries:

"Don't Fooley With Dooley"

"I'm a Hokie Devotee"

"Gobbler Gusto"

"If God Isn't a Hokie, Then Why Are Pumpkins Orange?"

"Ain't No Jokie To Be A Hokie"

"Gridfight at the Ho-Kay Corral"

"Be a Tech-Nician"

"Gig 'Em, Gobblers"

"Hassle 'Em, Hokies"

"Hokieland: Where Pigskin Isn't Just For Breakfast Anymore"

"Here Comes the Hokie Herd"

The winners, however were three different slogans: "Join the Dooley Dozen — 11 Players and You"; "Trek With Tech"; and a sports information office-generated entry, "Get In The Hokie Huddle."

Virginia Tech graduate and former cheerleader Kylene Barker won the 1979 Miss America contest.

GOING BIG-TIME When Lane Stadium was built in the mid-60s, blueprint plans allowed for possible expansion,

A packed Lane Stadium as it looked in 1996.

and the decision to add 12,500 permanent seats was made in 1975. Under Dooley, the expansion became reality. In 1980, Tech added 39 rows to the east stands, bringing Lane's capacity to 52,500, making it the largest stadium in Virginia.

1980: LOOKING PEACHY

Among the radio hits when Tech began its 1980 season on Sept. 6 at Wake Forest were "Sailing" by Christopher Cross and "All Out Of Love" by Air Supply.

Fans eagerly looked ahead to the 1980 season, and the opener at Wake Forest loomed large. The game saw a breakout performance by junior college transfer Robert Brown, a defensive end who sacked Wake Forest's All-ACC quarterback Jay Venuto four times. "We weren't sure about how good Robert really was," Tech defensive end John Gutekunst said, "until the first quarter." Tech won the first of four victories in a row, 16-7. The Hokies also whipped East Tennessee State (35-7), William & Mary (7-3) and James Madison (38-6) all in Blacksburg.

THE SOUND SILENCED TECH One of the most memorable near-wins in school history came on Oct. 4, 1980, at Clemson. The Hokies lost Cyrus Lawrence on the second play of the second quarter, but quarterback Steve Casey completed 23 of 40 passes for 208 yards to rally Tech from a 10-0 halftime deficit.

Three scoring tries were ruled short and Tech was assessed an illegal procedure penalty, the result of Casey's signals going unheard over the roar of a Death Valley Homecoming crowd of 64,000.

"We should have won the game," Dooley said. Instead the Tigers prevailed, 13-10, and Tech fell to 4-1.

FABRICATING SUCCESS? Six of the Hokies' eight wins that season came against schools that are now classified as Division I-AA — ETSU, William & Mary, JMU, Rhode Island, and VMI.

A WET, WILD, WONDERFUL WIN The '80 UVa showdown in Blacksburg on Oct. 18 marked Tech's first game using Lane Stadium's newly-expanded east stands, and 52,000 fans were on hand on a rainy day.

Those who could see clearly watched Cyrus Lawrence rush for 194 yards on a then-school record 40 carries. The Hokies upped their record to 6-1.

CAUGHT IN THE SPIDER WEB Next was Richmond, another Division I-AA school, but there would be no easy win on a rain-soaked, wind-whipped day. Spider halfback Barry Redden ran for 233 yards as UR upset Tech, 18-7, to drop the Hokies' record to 6-2.

Cornell wasn't the first Hokie player named Brown to dominate a game from the defensive end position. Robert, above, did it from 1980-81.

Super back Cyrus Lawrence saved his best performances for rival Virginia. In his last two games against the Cavaliers he gained 194 and 202 yards.

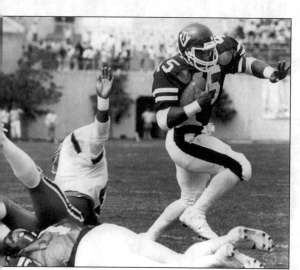

THE DROUGHT ENDS Dooley's Hokies then fell to Florida State, 31-7, but came back to whip VMI, 21-6. Thanks to the exploits of Brown, Johnson, Lawrence, wide receiver Sidney Snell, quarterback Steve Casey, linebacker Ashley Lee and defensive lineman Padro Phillips, Tech finished 8-3 and earned a bid to the Peach Bowl. It was the

BE LIKE MIKE

Linebacker Mike Johnson made his first career start in Tech's ninth game of the 1980 season, a 34-11 victory over West Virginia in Blacksburg on Nov. 1. A freshman who was originally thought to be an offensive line prospect, Johnson started in place of injured senior Lewis Stuart. Johnson would go on to have one of the greatest careers ever for a Hokie — on and off the field. As a senior he received the coveted Frank Loria Award; he earned a 3.5 grade point average in Tech's demanding architecture program; he earned second team All-America Academic Team honors; he was the Hokies' leading tackler

for two seasons; and he had a Pro Bowl NFL career, most of it with the Cleveland Browns.

Check out "Mike The Man's" incredible numbers:

1983 135 tackles (60 solo), 8 for loss; 3 sacks; 4 interceptions; 12 passes broken up.

1982 148 tackles (73 solo), 5 for loss; 2 sacks; 3 interceptions; 7 passes broken up.

1981 100 tackles (59 solo); 1 sack; 4 interceptions; 7 passes broken up.

1980 46 tackles (21 solo), 4 for loss; 2 interceptions.

That's six sacks, 13 interceptions and a mind-boggling 429 tackles in his career.

Teammates voted Mike Johnson — a product of DeMatha High School — Most Valuable Player for 1982.

Hokies' first postseason berth since 1968, and excitement was high. Tech took more than 14,000 fans to Atlanta, where the Hokies faced No. 18 Miami and quarterback Jim Kelly.

AT LEAST EVERYBODY HAD FUN The Hurricanes scored two touchdowns in the first 17 minutes then held off the Hokies for a 20-10 win in the Peach Bowl on Jan. 2, 1981. Tech closed to 14-10 midway through the third quarter, but was dogged by poor field position and penalties. Lawrence rushed for 134 yards on 27 carries and Ashley Lee had 15 tackles for Tech.

BUMMER Virginia Tech was 6-3 in 1981, and all it had to do was beat VMI to secure a second straight bowl bid. ABC-TV televised the game regionally from Blacksburg on a bitterly cold day (Nov. 21, 1981). A Hokie fumble set up VMI's lone score, and the Keydets had a 6-0 upset.

DOOLEY AGAINST UVA Tech took out its anger a week later against Virginia, winning 20-3 as Cyrus Lawrence rushed for 202 yards. That gave him a Tech single-season record 1,403.

The Tech-UVa series had been a hard-fought one since 1970; no matter what kind of season either team was having, fans never knew who was going to win when the two state rivals met. Tech had won five, lost four and tied one against the Wahoos in that span, and until the 1980 debacle none of the games were decided by more than 12 points. But that 30-0 Hokie win, followed by the decisive victory in '81, served notice to the Cavaliers that Tech intended things to change under Bill Dooley.

HOKIES QUIZ

10. When and where was Tech's first bowl appearance?

The expression on Virginia coach George Welsh's face gives you an idea of this Tech-UVa outcome. Bill Dooley pretty much had Welsh's number in the 1980s, beating him six of seven tries from 1980-86.

GUNNED DOWN AGAIN In just the second game of the 1982 season, Virginia Tech had a chance to atone for its Peach Bowl loss and the 1981 regular-season defeat (21-14) to Miami. Jim Kelly and the Hurricanes came to town on Sept. 18. A David Marvel tackle knocked Kelly out of action in the fourth quarter, but not before Kelly had completed 17 of 24 passes for 207 yards and a touchdown. The 'Canes prevailed, 14-8.

BEDEVILING COMEBACK One of the wildest wins in school history came on Oct. 9, 1982, at Durham, N.C., before a regional television audience. Duke led 21-0 for most of three quarters, and the Hokies still trailed, 21-14, with less than a minute to play. But with :33 left quarterback Todd Greenwood hit Allan Thomas for a 49-yard scoring pass, then threw a quick two-point conversion toss to tight end Mike Shaw to pull out a 22-21 win.

Tech registered three quarterback sacks in the second half and were led by linebacker James Robinson's 19-tackle performance.

FIRST NIGHT GAME This was one of the few state showdowns where a fan could sit just about anywhere he or she desired. The game was played on Thanksgiving night at the request of Ted Turner's cable superstation WTBS, and many Gobblers opted to stay home — and

Linebacker James "Rock" Robinson was one of Tech's great underrated players.

Tech's 1982 defensive unit ranked No. 1 nationally against the rush, allowing just 49.5 yards on the ground per game. Overall the Hokies ranked No. 8 in defense, allowing just 278.2 total yards per game.

warm — for Turkey Day and watch the game on TV.

It marked the first-ever game in Lane Stadium played under the lights. It was a chilly evening and hot chocolate sales were brisk. Tech won, 21-14, when quarterback Mark Cox scored from one yard out with 12:40 left.

1983: BRUCE BREAKS LOOSE

Virginia Tech fielded one of its greatest defensive squads ever in '83. The Hokies led the country in scoring defense (8.3 points per game) and rushing defense (69.4 yards per game) and ranked second in total defense (256.1 yards per game).

Junior defensive end Bruce Smith led the nation with 22 sacks and made five different All-America teams. In all he had 31 tackles behind the line of scrimmage for 223 yards in losses.

It was in 1983 that Smith — who picked Tech over Michigan and N.C. State — established himself as the most dominant force in college football.

THE 50 DEFENSE Tech's defense, using the five-man, or "50" front, was loaded. Smith and James Patterson were the tackles; Jesse Penn and David Marvel the ends; Orlando Williams the nose guard; James Robinson and Mike Johnson the linebackers; and Ashley Lee, Jake Clarke, Derek Carter and Bryan Burleigh the defensive backs. Seven of those players would sign pro contracts.

Tech's 1982 defensive unit ranked No. 1 nationally against the rush, allowing just 49.5 yards per game. Overall the Hokies ranked No. 8 in defense, allowing just 278.2 total yards per game.

Bruce Smith (78) is the greatest football player in Virginia Tech history.

THE STALLIONS Offensively, Tech's idea was to keep it on the ground. Two freshman tailbacks, Eddie Hunter and Maurice Williams, along with Otis Copeland and Desmar Becton, formed a stable of talented running backs that earned the nickname "The Stallions" from assistant coach Billy Hite. In 1983 Tech ranked fourth nationally in rushing offense (279 yards per game) thanks in large part to the blocking of bullish fullback Tony Paige.

Copeland led the way with 709 yards and seven touchdowns, followed by Williams (442, 4), Hunter (395, 4) Becton (371, 3) and Paige (366, 1).

WAKE-UP CALL Perhaps the opening game of the '83 season blew the Hokies' bowl chances. Wake Forest pulled the upset in Blacksburg, 13-6, even though Tech out-gained the Deacons 437-173. It was the Hokies' first

In Tech's 21-10 win over Vanderbilt, Ashley Lee intercepted two passes for touchdowns: one was an 88-yarder, the other a 94-yarder. In 1996, the yardage total stood as an NCAA record, as did his average yards per interception (91.0).

The 1983 West Virginia game didn't make Bill Dooley a happy man.

season-opening loss since 1978, and it would haunt them the rest of the season.

The Hokies then won four straight, over Memphis State (17-10), VMI (28-0), Louisville (31-0) and Duke (27-14). Smith sacked Blue Devil star quarterback Ben Bennett four times in the latter.

Offensive woes dogged Tech in a 13-0 loss at No. 4-ranked West Virginia on Oct. 15, in a game televised

48-0

There are three days Hokie fans will always remember: graduation day, their wedding day, and Nov. 19, 1983 — the day Tech could do no wrong.

It was a bright Saturday afternoon in Charlottesville, and the Tech-Virginia game was expected to be a close one. UVa was coming off an upset of North Carolina, and many observers believed the Wahoos were primed to beat Tech for the first time since 1979.

Tech didn't really know it at the time, but Virginia's upset of UNC effectively knocked the Hokies out of Peach Bowl consideration. Had the Tar Heels won they would've earned a

bigger bowl berth. With the loss, the Peach snatched them up. But Carolina said it didn't want to play the Hokies, so Tech was left out of the postseason.

"The preliminary bowl news pained the Hokies," wrote *Roanoke Times & World-News* columnist Bill Brill. "While they had won eight of 10, at best they were the backup team for a couple of post-season games.

"Unranked despite being 9-2 and unable to control their own destiny in a year in which many lesser teams already had bowls locked up, the Hokies took out their personal frustrations on helpless Virginia."

regionally by CBS.

The Hokies then won their next five games, topping off the season with one of the greatest wins in school history.

The crowd of 44,572 for Tech-UVa in 1983 set a Scott Stadium record. Those fans saw the most lopsided victory in the 65-game history of the series, 34-0.

THIS WAS THEIR BOWL GAME As it turned out, any game played after the 1983 season-finale against Virginia would have been anticlimactic. Tech shellacked the 'Hoos, 48-0. Fans rushed the field in a wild celebration after the game, as Hokie students tore down a Scott Stadium goal post and paraded it around Rugby Road that evening.

"Everything the Hokies did was right," wrote Bill Brill in the Sunday, Nov. 20, *Roanoke Times & World-News*. "Everything UVa did was wrong. The result was the Battle of the Little Big Horn revisited. George Welsh was

Being a first-team All-America was OK with Bruce Smith.

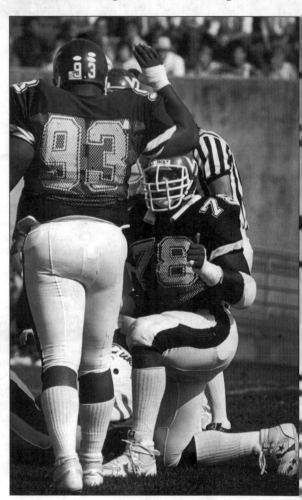

Tailback Maurice Williams breaks free for a long scoring jaunt against UVa in 1983.

an unwilling Gen. George Custer."

It was the "Day of the Stallions," as Tech amassed 507 yards of total offense. Maurice Williams galloped for 97 yards and two touchdowns — on just three carries (an average of 32.3 yards per carry). Eddie Hunter had seven carries for 83 yards and a touchdown. Otis Copeland carried 13 times for 61 yards and a score. Ricky Bailey had 10 carries for 28 yards and two touchdowns, while Desmar Becton had seven carries for 22 yards.

Tech had four interceptions and four sacks. So effective was the Hokie defense that Virginia never moved into Tech territory until late in the third period, with the Hokies on top, 34-0.

By that time, according to a story by Doug Doughty in the Nov. 20 *Roanoke Times*, Virginia's banged-up bench "looked like Beirut."

Tech's nine wins in 1983 marked the most for a Hokie team since 1905. Its four shutouts were the most since the 1938 season.

HONORED HOKIES Several Hokies earned postseason honors in '83. Smith was a Kodak First Team All-America pick; Mike Johnson was an Associated Press Honorable Mention All-America selection; and Derek Carter and punter David Cox were both named second-team All-South.

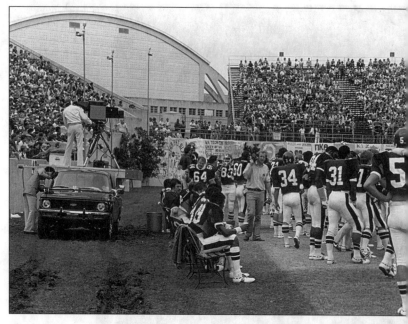

Virginia Tech's television appearances went way up during the Bill Dooley years.

Bruce Smith graced the first-ever issue of The Hokie Huddler *on May 22, 1984.*

Tech introduced its new streamlined "VT" logo on Sept. 8, 1984, for its game at Wake Forest.

1984: BACK TO A BOWL

With 13 returning starters from its 9-2 squad, Virginia Tech expected to field a strong team in 1984. In part to capitalize on the growing enthusiasm, Tech introduced *The Hokie Huddler* on May 22, 1984.

Maybe he was sick of the state's newspapers ripping his program. Maybe he thought Tech needed self-promotion. At any rate, Bill Dooley decided the Hokies needed its own sports newspaper, and he hired former *Collegiate Times* editor-in-chief and *Roanoke Times* reporter Doug Waters for the job.

In the season-opener, Wake Forest led Tech, 20-14, and had the ball at the Hokies' 3-yard line. A motion penalty and a 15-yard sack by end Cornell Urquhart forced Wake to attempt a field goal, which sailed wide right. From there, the Hokies took possession at their 20-yard line. Ten plays later, Eddie Hunter scored from five yards out with 2:08 left to give Tech a 21-20 lead. Deacon placekicker Doug Illing missed a 40-yard field goal attempt by inches on the game's final play.

Said Waters: "I remember sitting in the press box and thinking, 'If we lose to Wake Forest, it's going to kill any hopes of getting *The Hokie Huddler* off the ground.' "

GREAT IN STATE In one of his first columns, Waters wrote that the Hokies were "leaving the state teams behind." He had a point: In the last four seasons Tech had

Bruce Smith and friends dominated state teams like William & Mary in the 1980s.

outscored state opponents Virginia, VMI, Richmond and William & Mary by a combined 435-101.

But Virginia decided it was time to catch up. On a gray, overcast "Bleaksburg" day (Sept. 29), the Cavaliers atoned for the year's previous embarrassment with a 26-23 win at Lane Stadium. Trailing, 23-13, and facing a fourth-and-1 situation from the Tech 34-yard line, UVa freshman receiver John Ford made a fingertip catch to set up a fourth-quarter touchdown, and the Wahoos scored on their next possession to pull out the win — one that springboarded them to a Peach Bowl berth.

Tech's defense ranked second nationally in scoring defense, second in rushing defense and third in total defense in 1984.

MAROON MONSOON In an Oct. 6 game against VMI in Norfolk, the 2-2 Hokies wore maroon pants for the first-time ever in the modern era. Tech won, 54-7. *Hokie Huddle* editor Doug Waters deemed the white-jersey/maroon-pants ensembles Tech's "Lucky Outfits." Tech followed that with wins over Duke (27-0), William & Mary (38-14), Temple (9-7) and Tulane (13-6) to run its record to 7-2 as it prepared to take on Clemson in Death Valley.

HOKIES QUIZ

SMITH FIGHTS FOR INDEPENDENCE After the Hokies' 17-10 loss at Clemson, they defeated Vanderbilt 23-3 to secure an Independence Bowl berth.

"We sort of feel like we're on a roll," Tech President William Lavery said, referring to Smith's accomplishment and Tech's bowl bid. Then things started to unravel.

11. How many bowl games have the Hokies played in?

Because of his fight with the NCAA, Bruce Smith was the center of attention at the 1984 Independence Bowl.

OUTLANDISH TALENT

Strange as it sounds now — after following their respective pro careers — but William "The Refrigerator" Perry of Clemson was considered Bruce Smith's equal as a defensive lineman for most of 1984. Tech played Clemson that season on Nov. 10, and *Greensboro Daily News* columnist Wilt Browning — one of eight men who voted for that year's Outland Trophy — was in the press box. Clemson won, 17-10, in Tech's next-to-last regular-season game. Although Smith had nine tackles (eight solo) to Perry's six (four solo), Browning wrote that Perry had outplayed Smith. "Perry may have just then clinched the Outland Trophy as the nation's best lineman," wrote Browning in a column titled "The day belonged to Perry."

But apparently Browning changed his mind, because on Thursday, Dec. 7, Smith — who finished the year with 16 sacks and 52 solo tackles — became the first football player from a Virginia school to win the Outland.

Browning later said he voted for Smith because in four years at Tech he accounted for losses totaling more than five times the length of a football field (504 yards).

It was big news in Blacksburg because it proved a player could go to Tech and still be in the limelight. Tech was beginning to shed its small-time image.

The greatness of Smith's Hokie career was secured in the spring of 1985 when the Buffalo Bills made him the No. 1 pick in the NFL Draft.

A year and a half earlier, the NCAA deemed Bruce Smith and seven other players ineligible for postseason play because of some minor rules infractions. Apparently a Tech coach had made an illegal contact with Smith, while an alumnus sent a load of firewood to Smith's ailing father. The other seven players were cleared after ensuing appeals, but not Smith.

The Hokies were 3 1/2 point favorites to beat Air Force in the 1984 Independence Bowl.

Dooley kept the matter quiet. When the story broke, it was big news. Would the Independence Bowl have tendered Tech the offer had it known its star player was ineligible? Why wasn't anyone told of the situation?

Smith took the case to court. He said he had done nothing wrong and deserved to play in his first — and only — bowl game. Judge Kenneth Devore ruled in favor of Smith. Irate, the NCAA threatened to pull its sanction from the Independence Bowl, which would effectively eliminate the game. The next day bowl chairman Dr. Cecil Lloyd wrote a letter to the NCAA saying it would abide by the NCAA's edict.

So Smith filed another suit, this time in Caddo Parish Circuit Court in Shreveport, La. That judge agreed that Smith had not been given due process and should be

Bruce Smith edged Clemson's William "The Refrigerator" Perry for the 1984 Outland Trophy.

12. In the 1986 Peach Bowl, Chris Kinzer's game-winning kick was set up by a penalty. Name the penalty and the two players involved.

allowed to play.

The NCAA urged the Independence Bowl to take the matter to a Louisiana Court of Appeals, but the three-judge panel refused to hear any arguments. The panel's ruling said in part: "The original violations were relatively minor, the probationary sanctions directed at the school have long since expired, the sanctions against other Virginia Tech athletes were removed, and Smith is the only athlete in the entire country singled out as ineligible for post-season play."

The whole ridiculous scenario did nothing but make everyone involved look bad. Instead of reveling in the glory of an Outland Trophy and his first bowl game, Smith endured press conferences and probing questions. Perhaps because of all the distractions, the Hokies played poorly and were defeated by Air Force, 23-7.

THEY DIDN'T KNOW ANY BETTER College football players of today may receive up to $300 worth of bowl gifts from their respective schools. They get sweat suits, golf shirts, windbreakers, Starter jackets, sweatshirts, shoes, watches, bags, T-shirts, shorts — you name it.

Tech received a guarantee of $425,000 for the 1984 Independence Bowl.

That wasn't the case in 1984. "We got these white V-neck sweaters, a watch, and this little gym bag that could barely hold your shoes, and that was it," said cornerback Derek Carter, now an administrator at Tech. "We thought that was great."

Bruce Smith celebrates his elite status as the NFL's No. 1 draft pick with his nephew, Kevin Smith.

1985: STRONG FINISH

The Hokies lost their first three games and four of their first five. Tech entered the Virginia game with a 2-4 record and was a 10-point underdog. The oddsmakers looked like geniuses after the first half, as Virginia led, 10-0. It looked like sales for the "Dump Dooley" T-shirts advertised in area newspapers would skyrocket.

In Tech's locker room at halftime, Dooley decided to go back to the basics. Instead of panicking and trying to come back all at once, he urged his players to be patient.

Taking advantage of the superior strength and experience of its senior-laden offensive line, Tech began ramming the ball into the heart of Virginia's defense. The Hokies ran on 35 of their first 44 plays of the second half, getting blocks of yardage with each burst.

"We decided that if we were going to lose, we were at least going to make Virginia pay for it," said center Mark Johnson.

Tech ran off an 18-play, 80-yard drive, with no gain more than nine yards. It ate up seven minutes and gave the Hokies defense a nice rest.

Tech scored on its second, third and fourth possessions of the second half and won easily, 28-10. A highlight of the comeback was a third-quarter run by Eddie Hunter where he spun, drop-stepped, high-stepped and even pedaled backwards for a big gain.

Florida was one of the better teams on Bill Dooley's football schedules. The Gators won the 1985 contest 35-18 in Gainesville.

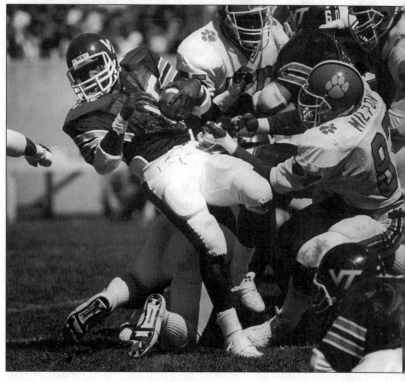

Tailback Eddie Hunter shows off his trademark "I'll Run Backwards If I Have To" style against Clemson.

How did Howell catch the Hail Mary of '85?

HAIL, YES The Hokies hadn't effectively used a "Hail Mary" play since Ron Zollicoffer's grab in 1978, so they were due. It came against Memphis State in Blacksburg on Nov. 2, 1985. Leading 10-7, quarterback Mark Cox heaved a 47-yard pass into the end zone, where wingback Terrence Howell came down with the ball.

"Allan Thomas went up for it, and as he did, I yelled for him to tip it my way," Howell said. "All of a sudden the ball was in front of me, and I cupped it against my chest. It happened so fast, it surprised me."

Tech won the game, 31-10, beat Louisville, 41-17, and Vanderbilt, 38-24, to finish 6-5 — an off year, but a winning campaign nonetheless.

1986: A BOWL WIN

There were no real signs that 1986 was going to be a special year for Virginia Tech football. Even *The Hokie Huddler* predicted a 6-5 campaign. The Hokies had lost all five starters from their offensive line and would be testing a new quarterback. At least Tech would have a single signal caller. After four years of rotating Mark Cox and Todd Greenwood, the Hokies were going with one guy: Erik Chapman.

CINCY MADE TECH WINCE

The Hokies had a recent pattern of season-opening woes. A year earlier they had lost at Cincinnati, 31-14; two years before, Wake Forest beat Tech, 13-6. Now the Bearcats were back again.

Tech lost an early scoring opportunity when tight end Steve Johnson fumbled deep in Bearcat territory — but appeared to be out of bounds. The ball skirted out of the end zone, and officials ruled a touchback. Instead of Tech having the ball at the Cincinnati 5-yard line, the Bearcats took over at the 20.

Placekicker Chris Kinzer — who would go on to have his greatest season — missed two makable field goals. Still, Tech led 20-13 late in the game.

On fourth-and-5, Cincinnati tried a pass that was tipped not once but twice by Tech cornerback Eddie Neel. But he couldn't knock it down, and Bearcat Scott Tackett snared it from the air and ran it to the Hokie 26-yard line. Tackett then caught a 7-yard scoring pass from quarterback Danny McCoin with :14 left. UC won, 24-20.

COME ON DOWN!

It all turned around a week later as the Hokies ventured into Clemson's Death Valley in a game televised on the ACC network. Tech was a two-touchdown underdog and had lost nine straight to the Tigers.

Memorial Stadium was rocking on a hot, sun-washed afternoon. The Clemson band was blaring and the crowd was screaming. "It was an incredibly intimidating place," defensive end Morgan Roane said. "All you could see

There would be no more quarterback controversy when Erik Chapman took over as Tech's signal-caller in 1986.

Paul Nelson would not be intimidated by Clemson's Death Valley

was orange, and all you could hear was noise."

As per tradition, Clemson's players stood at the top of the Memorial Stadium hill, rubbing "Howard's Rock" — named after Tiger legend Frank Howard — before taking the field.

"Look at that," linebacker Paul Nelson said, talking to his cohort-in-crime, Lawrence White. "Let's wave their [butts] down here. Bring 'em on!" White thought for a minute. "Yeah, that would look good on television," he said. So Nelson and White started gesturing toward the Tigers, and pretty soon the whole team joined in.

"We wanted to show those people we weren't scared," Roane said.

Clemson sports information director Bob Bradley said he had never seen anything like it. The stunt upset Dooley. "I don't like that," he said. "If you do something like that, you better be able to back it up."

Back it up they did. Kinzer kicked field goals of 31 and 38 yards, Mitch Dove recovered a blocked punt in the end zone for a score, and Chapman found Johnson for a 5-yard scoring pass to pull the 20-14 upset in front of 77,000 fans. The Hokies were 1-1.

The 1985 team became the first in school history to post a winning season after an 0-3 start.

The news that Bill Dooley would not return as Tech's coach for 1987 made big news prior to the Hokies' game at Syracuse. Here a television camera captures Dooley during the Friday workout at the Carrier Dome.

Erik Chapman raises his helmet in victory at Syracuse.

NEVER A DULL MOMENT Everyone in Hokieland was riding high after the big Clemson upset in 1986. Then, once again, Tech's program was mired in controversy. On Thursday afternoon after practice prior to the Hokies' third game of the season, at Syracuse, Dooley told his players he had been fired by the university, effective at the end of the season.

The players were stunned. They had no clue anything was wrong, but the situation had been brewing for at least a year.

In the fall of 1985, the *Roanoke Times & World-News* chronicled Tech's financial woes. A multi-part series by sportswriter Jack Bogaczyk revealed that many of the athletic association's problems could be traced to Dooley's dual role as athletic director and head football coach.

In late February of 1986, President William Lavery advised Dooley that his deal as athletic director/head football coach would be terminated at the end of the

Tech President William Lavery wanted to separate Bill Dooley's dual roles.

13. *Two Tech assistant coaches have coached in Hokie bowl games under different head coaches. Name them and the coaches.*

1986 season. Dooley had previously signed a contract that called for him to coach until Jan. 1, 1989, and act as athletic director until January 1994.

Dooley claimed breach of contract and filed a $3.5 million lawsuit against the university.

Then news shocked Dooley's players, who affectionately called him "The Bull." They loved him.

"I remember when we first moved into NUF [New Undergraduate Facility]," linebacker Lawrence White said. "We told him, 'Coach, you gotta get us an ice cream machine in the dining hall.' Well, he loved ice cream, so a week later there sat this beautiful Dairy Queen machine: vanilla, chocolate and vanilla/chocolate swirl. We thought he was the greatest."

FIRED UP Unfazed by the media circus swirling around them, the Hokies went out and beat the Orangemen in the Carrier Dome, 26-17, on Sept. 20. Tailback Maurice Williams gained a season-high 159 yards, while fellow tailback Eddie Hunter added 125 as Tech tallied a season-high 486 yards of total offense. "The news motivated us," free safety Carter Wiley said. "This is just one of eight more we're going to win for him. We want to show the university they made a mistake." Tech was 2-1.

Carter Wiley and the rest of the Hokie players wanted Tech's administration to regret firing their beloved coach.

AND THEN, REALITY SET IN Even after a few weeks had passed, the Dooley story was still big news. It was beginning to wear on some players. "I'm ready for this thing to die down," linebacker Jamel Agemy said. "It seems like every time a reporter talks to us, the first four or five questions are about football, then the next 30 questions are about Coach Dooley. Hey, he's not coming back. That's all there is to it."

In early October, Lavery announced that the university had reached an out-of-court settlement with Dooley, worth about $650,000.

The Hokies' 1986 wins at Clemson and Syracuse marked their first back-to-back road victories since 1974.

SPELL IT OUT Tech rolled off two more wins (37-10 over East Tennessee State and 37-10 over West Virginia) before a short midseason slump. There was a 27-27 tie at home against South Carolina.

Tech then traveled to Norfolk to meet Temple, a team coached by former Hokie quarterback Bruce Arians. Star tailback Paul Palmer rushed 44 times for 239 yards as Temple upset Tech, 29-13, in the 40th annual Oyster Bowl. The Owls later forfeited the win when Palmer was ruled ineligible.

But the Hokies (4-2-1) didn't know that at the time, and figured they had to win their four remaining games to earn a bowl bid.

"After that loss, we wrote our last four opponents on the blackboard," Wiley said. "For every win, we'd get a

Tech seemingly had Paul Palmer surrounded, but still couldn't stop him.

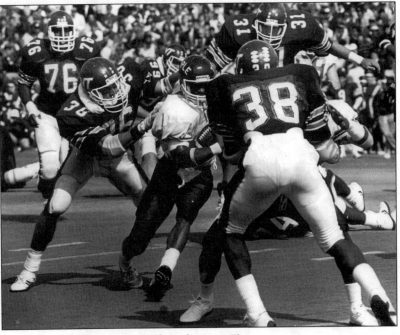

Maurice Williams led Tech in rushing from 1984-86 and gained 1,029 yards in the Hokies' Peach Bowl championship season. He averaged 5.42 yards per carry during his career.

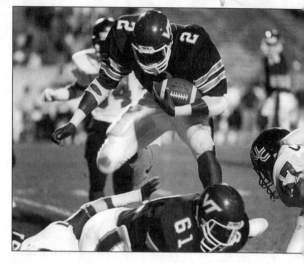

letter. Our goal was to spell B-O-W-L."

A Kentucky player lies stunned in disbelief as the Hokies go wild. Chris Kinzer's 49-yard field goal with one second left gave Tech a 17-15 victory.

On Oct. 25, Tech whipped Virginia, 42-10, continuing Dooley's domination of the Wahoos. Since 1980, Tech had won six of the seven games by an average score of 30-9. This time the win was for more than just state bragging rights; Peach Bowl scout Frank Stiteler was in the press box, and said Tech had to win to be considered for his Dec. 31 bowl game. Maurice Williams was the star with 143 yards and two touchdowns on 18 carries. Eddie Hunter carried 25 times for 130 yards and two scores as Tech improved to 5-2-1.

Chris Kinzer was "The Man" in 1986.

'THE HALF-MILLION DOLLAR KICK' One of the most memorable games of a memorable 1986 season came on Nov. 1 in Blacksburg against Kentucky — and former Tech coach Jerry Claiborne. On a rainy, overcast day, sophomore placekicker Chris Kinzer kicked a 49-yard field goal with one second left to give the Hokies a 17-15 win and boost their record to 6-2-1.

Kentucky's Mark Logan ran three yards for a score with 4:20 to play to give the Wildcats a 15-14 lead. Eddie Hunter fumbled the ensuing kickoff out-of-bounds at the 5-yard line. He atoned for his mistake by gaining three yards on fourth-and-1 from the Tech 9-yard line.

Tech was faced with fourth-and-3 from its own 43. "In the huddle, I said, 'Peach Bowl,' " said Chapman, "then I called the play."

"The play" was a pass to fullback Earnie Jones, good for 12 yards. The Hokies' bowl hopes remained alive. A 9-yard pass to Steve Johnson and an 8-yard Hunter draw got Tech within Kinzer's range, but time was running down and the Hokies were out of timeouts.

Despite the slick, muddy footing and the ticking clock, Kinzer calmly jogged out to the field, and put his tee down.

"When I looked up, the clock was at eight seconds and running," he said. "I looked at Steve [Hale, Tech's snapper] and he motioned me to move up. I had set my tee too far back, but Steve recognized it right away. So I ran back to the tee and set it in the right place."

Then he booted the 49-yarder with one second to spare.

"It helped that we were facing the scoreboard," Kinzer said. "Ideally, I wanted to work it so when the ball went

HOKIES QUIZ

14. What was the score of the 1993 Independence Bowl with 35 seconds left in the first half?

NFL All-Pro kicker Mark Moseley gave Chris Kinzer his first kicking shoe.

HOKIES QUIZ

15. What inanimate object did the 1995 Tech defense take with it wherever it went?

through, there wouldn't have been any time left. But Steve snapped it with six seconds left."

Hale might've been thinking more of himself than Kinzer when he told him to move up. "When he was seven yards away, I could always get the laces to come up on the ball, away from him," Hale said. "But when he was 7 ½ yards away, I couldn't get the laces to come up."

The kick, Kinzer's 16th of the year, broke Dave Strock's school record for most field goals in a season. It was also worth about $500,000, the Peach Bowl payoff. Bowl scout Frank Stiteler said if Tech had lost it would have been out of the running for his bowl game.

"Surely it is clear that Dooley's final edition at Tech, if not his best, is his grittiest," wrote *Roanoke Times & World-News* columnist Bill Brill after the game. "The Hokies might not be that good, but they don't know it."

.44 MAGNUM A straight-on kicker in the mold of Mark Moseley, Chris Kinzer of Dublin, Va., was the leading field goal kicker in Division I-A for 1986. His right leg provided the winning or tying margin in seven Hokie games. He made 24 of 29 field goal attempts and converted a school-record 17 kicks in a row — all with a square-toed white Nike high-topped shoe with thick brown-and-yellow laces that would look more at home on a pair of hiking boots. Because his foot was so powerful, Kinzer stenciled ".44" on the left side of the shoe in maroon letters and "Magnum" on the right side.

The shoe cost $275, but Kinzer wanted two. "So Nike gave me a deal: two for $500," he said.

Kinzer attributed much of his success to holder Jeff Ballance and snapper Steve Hale, called "The Banjo Boys."

Kinzer said the story behind the nickname was "kind of dumb."

Hale, who was just 5-foot-8, 198 pounds, was small for a center, so his teammates jokingly called him "Big Bubba" after a pro wrestler. "Then that got shortened to 'B.B.', as in B.B. King, the famous blues guitarist," Kinzer said. "Then the guitar evolved into a banjo."

To keep loose during games, the three would pretend to play imaginary banjos on the sideline.

CLAPP FOR THESE GUYS Part of the reason for Tech's surprising success in '86 was the development of its offensive line. All five starters from 1985 were gone, and two projected starters — Bill Cox and Stacey Johnson — were lost because of academics and injuries.

Still, the rag-tag crew of Mike Clapp, Bob Frulla, Kevin Keeffe, Todd Grantham and Jim Davie got the job done.

"They don't have the body frames or the strength of

Give him a hand: Mike Clapp got the job done anyway possible.

some of the guys we had last year," tailback Maurice Williams said. "But they're a lot dirtier.

"Look at Clapp. You have to hit him with a baseball bat to really beat him."

HAPPY DAY Tech finished the regular season with a 17-10 win over Richmond on Nov. 8 and a 29-21 victory over Vanderbilt Nov. 15. A week later executive director Lee Ayres and scout Frank Stiteler traveled to Blacksburg to officially extend the Hokies an offer to play in the Peach Bowl.

Excited by the prospect of going bowling, Tech's players — with the help from the promotions department — put together a rap video titled "The New Peach Bowl Step." The video captured the fun-loving, hell-raising, devil-may-care spirit of the '86 Hokies.

N.C. State quarterback Erik Kramer was named the '86 Peach Bowl MVP because bowl officials prodded media members to turn in their ballots early.

Bill Dooley officially accepts Tech's 1986 Peach Bowl invitation.

Sports Illustrated
*named Chris Kinzer
its Offensive Player
of the Bowls for
1986.*

THE PEACH BOWL With Bruce Smith decked out in a lush
fur coat on the sidelines, Virginia Tech rallied from a
21-10 halftime deficit to beat N.C. State, 25-24, in one of
the most exciting Peach Bowls ever.

Tech turned two Erik Kramer fumbles into
touchdowns in the second half. Carter Wiley recovered
the first on his own 28-yard line, and the Hokies ran off a
15-yard drive capped by a one-yard plunge by Williams.
The two-point conversion failed.

Tech took over on the second fumble around midfield
to open the fourth quarter. Eleven plays later Chapman hit
Johnson with a six-yard scoring pass to give the Hokies a
22-21 lead. Another two-point conversion was stopped.

Mike Cofer's 33-yard field goal gave the Wolfpack a
24-22 lead with 7:12 remaining, and the Wolfpack had
the momentum when Kelly Hollodick faked a punt and
ran for a crucial first down at the Hokie 35-yard line. But
Jamel Agemy kept Tech's hopes alive with back-to-back
tackles behind the line of scrimmage, and two plays later

*Bruce Smith was
toasty warm on the
sidelines in Atlanta.*

Wingback Dave Everett helped set up one of the biggest plays in Hokie history.

State was forced to punt from the Tech 41-yard line. The ball went into the end zone. Starting from its own 20, Tech had 1:53 to pull the game out.

The Hokies moved the ball to the State 36-yard line, but time was running out and Tech was out of timeouts. Then, the Hokies ran a pitch right to Maurice Williams, who was tackled behind the line of scrimmage by N.C. State cornerback Derrick Taylor for a one-yard loss.

"I got hit on the shin and my leg cramped up," Williams said. "then [Tech's people on the sidelines] told me just to stay there."

Because of the "injury," the officials stopped the clock with 27 seconds remaining.

Facing fourth-and-three with 37 seconds left, Tech could've tried a 54-yard field goal. Kinzer's career-best was a 50-yarder. Although Kinzer tried to talk him into kicking it, Dooley opted to go for the first down. But he didn't call the play; he left that to Chapman, who called "Quick Orange 48."

"The play was designed for me to roll out right," Chapman said. "If the defensive end stayed back I was going to run for it. He came up, so I threw."

And tight end Steve Johnson caught it for nine yards to the State 28, getting out of bounds with 15 seconds left.

Even with no timeouts left, Dooley decided against

The crowd of 53,668 at the 1986 Peach Bowl was the third-highest in bowl history at the time. Tech took a then school-record 16,000 fans to the event.

The Kick.

trying a 45-yarder and instead wanted one more shot at the end zone. Chapman missed wingback David Everett, but Tech was called for holding anyway. Now the ball was at the 39 with 11 seconds left. A 56-yarder would have been pushing it for Kinzer.

The pressure was on. Chapman rolled left with the option to throw to either Everett or split end Donald Wayne Snell. Facing man-to-man coverage, Chapman chose Everett, who had beaten State safety Brian Gay, a third-team substitute, on the left sideline. Gay recovered enough to be called for interference at the 2-yard line. The 15-yard penalty pushed the ball to the State 24,

Steve Johnson made one of the biggest catches of the '86 Peach Bowl.

setting up Kinzer's winning field goal.

"There was no doubt about the call," Everett said. "If he doesn't grab me, I score the winning touchdown. That made me mad, because before the game my sister told me she would give me all of her Christmas money if I caught a touchdown pass in the Peach Bowl. When I saw the ball coming, all I could think about was all that cash."

Gay said he barely touched Everett.

"I might have brushed the side of him but I don't think I was leaning on him," Gay said.

There was no decision to make now. Dooley sent Kinzer in for the 40-yarder. State called a timeout to ice him, to no avail. Kinzer simply dropped to one knee, propped his chin on his left hand, chewed his gum and gave Dooley a wink. Dooley winked back.

A reporter later asked him what he was thinking about. "I make it a point," Kinzer said. "I never think."

He never saw the ball go through the uprights, either.

"After I made the field goal against Kentucky the team jumped all over me and I was down on the bottom and I couldn't breathe," Kinzer said. "It really scared me. I thought I was going to get suffocated beneath a pile of maniacs. So I got the hell out of Dodge and didn't stop until I got to the locker room."

Well, he did take time en route to make a few gestures to the N.C. State bench. "Just shootin' 'em down," he said.

Roanoke Hokie fans appreciated what Bill Dooley accomplished during his run.

1987-1994
The Beamer Years

Frank Beamer had to overcome many obstacles during his early years at Tech.

Frank Beamer's first two seasons were stormy ones for the Hokies, as illustrated in this Huddler cartoon by George Wills.

Two days before Christmas 1986, new Virginia Tech Athletic Director Dutch Baughman announced that Murray State's Frank Beamer would succeed Bill Dooley as the Hokies' new football coach.

In his first news conference, Beamer said his offensive philosophy came from Bobby Ross and his defensive philosophy came from Jerry Claiborne.

He would implement those philosophies under less than ideal conditions. Under Dooley, Tech's football program had exceeded the NCAA 30 per year, 95 at any one time scholarship rule by 32 over a three-year period, and the NCAA issued heavy sanctions. During the 1988-89, 1989-90 and 1990-91 seasons no more than 85 student-athletes in football could be on scholarship. Tech could sign no more than 17 recruits for 1988-89.

Beamer also had to overcome increased academic standards and an upgraded schedule. The combination of those factors made for hard times, but Beamer kept the faith and turned his program around. After going a combined 11-21-1 his first three years, Beamer went 27-9 in his last three, played in an unprecedented three straight bowls and won two bowls, including the 1995 Sugar Bowl.

BUMMER OF A SEASON *The Hokie Huddler* predicted a 6-5 record for Beamer's inaugural 1987 campaign. Then Tech lost several key starters for the entire year: Defensive tackle Horacio Moronta, outside linebacker Sean Lucas, tailback Tyrone Branch and cornerback Mitch Dove were academic casualties, while linebacker Jamel Agemy, linebacker Lawrence White and offensive lineman Stacy Johnson were lost for the season with preseason injuries. Wingback David Everett missed most of the year with a shoulder injury.

Tech's remaining players had trouble adjusting to the new wide-tackle six defensive alignment, and the year was a disaster. The Hokies finished 2-9, beating only Navy and Cincinnati.

Horacio Moronta was one of many key losses Tech suffered in 1987.

TOUGH TIMES Things didn't get much better in 1988. Beamer was allowed to sign just 13 newcomers, he started a freshman quarterback and faced a schedule that would be ranked toughest in the nation. The Hokies' opponents had a combined winning percentage of .673, and Tech finished the season 3-8.

VIRGINIA HAD MOORE The '88 Tech-UVa game in Blacksburg was marked by an intentionally tasteless performance by those jocular satirists, the Virginia Pep Band, who made fun of United States Olympian basketball player Bimbo Coles, a Tech student-athlete. The band also exceeded its allotted time by two minutes, delaying the featured guest, Governor Gerald Baliles.

Bimbo Coles was the target of the UVa Pep Band's derision in 1988.

Cavalier Herman Moore caught seven passes for 175 yards as Virginia won, 16-10. The irritating thing about his performance was that Tech had recruited him heavily. Moore, in fact, was ready to sign with the Hokies

Mickey got his kicks against WVU in '89.

FRANK BEAMER PLAYERS DRAFTED BY NFL IN THE 1990S

1990 Outside linebacker Jock Jones, eighth round, Cleveland; cornerback Roger Brown, eighth round, Green Bay.

1991 Defensive end Al Chamblee, 12th round, Tampa Bay.

1992 Offensive tackle Eugene Chung, first round, New England; quarterback Will Furrer, fourth round, Chicago; free safety Damien Russell, sixth round, San Francisco; offensive guard William Boatwright, seventh round, Philadelphia; cornerback John Granby, 12th round, Denver.

1993 None. (Vaughn Hebron signed a free-agent contract with Philadelphia).

1994 Cornerback Tyronne Drakeford, second round, San Francisco; tight end John Burke, fourth round, New England; center Jim Pyne, seventh round, Tampa Bay.

1995 Wide receiver Antonio Freeman, third round, Green Bay; linebacker Ken Brown, fourth round, Denver.

1996 Wide receiver Bryan Still, second round, San Diego; defensive tackle J.C. Price, third round, Carolina.

Don Heinrich's College Football publication predicted a 3-8 season for the Hokies in 1989.

after his official visit, but, according to *Hoos 'N Hokies, The Rivalry* by Doug Doughty and Roland Lazenby, he read in the *Richmond Times-Dispatch* that Tech would not accept partial qualifiers. He had not yet qualified on the SAT. Virginia looked at Moore's transcripts and figured he would make it, which he did, and offered him a scholarship. Moore went on to catch 17 passes for 505 yards in three games against the Hokies.

A 'MAJOR' ACCOMPLISHMENT From 1973-1989, Tech defeated West Virginia just four times. Entering the 1989 season, the Mountaineers had built a 23-10-1 lead in the series, and it seemed as if the Hokies would never win in Morgantown.

That changed on Oct. 7, 1989, as Tech beat No. 9 West Virginia, 12-10, before a homecoming crowd of 62,563. The Hokies were 16-point underdogs and were playing without three of their best players: starting quarterback Will Furrer, who had torn ligaments in his knee a week earlier against Temple; starting tailback Jon Jeffries; and future NFL cornerback Roger Brown.

Virginia Tech's 12-10 win over No. 9 West Virginia in 1989 was its first over a Top 10 team in 25 years.

But quarterback Cam Young completed 15 of 22 passes for 167 yards — despite playing with what he later learned was a torn rotator cuff — and placekicker Mickey Thomas booted four field goals.

"I knew I was going to have a good day after testing

the turf Friday afternoon," said Thomas, like Kinzer a straight-on placekicker. "The difference between kicking on artificial turf and natural grass is like hitting a golf shot in the fairway instead of the rough."

Tech intercepted West Virginia quarterback Major Harris twice and allowed only 185 yards of total offense for the day.

The win was Tech's first in Morgantown in 22 years and began a distinctive turn in the series: The Hokies would go on to win five of the next seven games with WVU, including a 34-6 rout in 1994 and 27-0 shutout in Morgantown in 1995.

"We've beaten a really good football team and a great football program today," Beamer said. "We have a tremendous amount of respect for Don Nehlen and his football program. It says a lot about what we've been able to accomplish at Tech to win a game like this here again this year. I'm proud of our team because I know we've competed with and defeated one of the top programs in the country."

Tech's defense ranked third nationally in rushing defense and fourth in total defense in 1989.

DON'T DOUBT THOMAS A few weeks after his West Virginia exploits, Thomas would set a school record for field goals in one game when he connected on six against Vanderbilt, an 18-0 Hokie win.

HEART OF THE MATTER Beamer suffered chest pains during Tech's 14-10 loss at East Carolina on Oct. 21, a game in which tailbacks Vaughn Hebron (135) and Tony Kennedy (114) both ran for more than 100 yards but the Hokies could manage just one touchdown.

Beamer underwent a transluminal coronary angioplasty the following Wednesday to relieve what was 90-95 percent blockage of an artery leading to his heart.

A pack-and-a-half-a-day smoker during the season, Beamer quit the habit and has been healthy ever since.

He missed Tech's ensuing game with Tulane on Oct. 28, but Billy Hite led the Hokies to a 30-13 win.

Billy Hite, the assistant who filled in during Frank Beamer's illness, was 1-0 as a head coach at Tech.

A KNOCKOUT SERIES The Virginia game (Nov. 11) was the backdrop for shenanigans once again in '89. The No. 18 Cavaliers, a nine-point favorite, led 24-0 at halftime. But the Hokies, behind third-string quarterback Rodd Wooten, staged a mad comeback, scoring the game's last 17 points. Tech had the ball with less than two minutes to play, but UVa's Jason Wallace intercepted a Wooten pass to preserve a 32-25 win.

Things got out of control at the final gun and a fracas broke out. Beamer rushed into the melee to break things up and caught an unintentional elbow from Hokie end Jimmy Whitten, now an assistant strength and

ALL 1980s TEAM

The *Hokie Huddler* readers voted the following All-1980s Virginia Tech Football Team:

OFFENSE
Quarterback: Steve Casey
Tailback: Cyrus Lawrence
Fullback: Tony Paige
Wingback: Sidney Snell
Split end: Myron Richardson
Tight end: Steve Johnson
Offensive tackle: Wally Browne
Offensive tackle: Todd Grantham
Offensive guard: Kent Thomas
Offensive guard: Tom Mehr
Center: Mark Johnson

Punter: Dave Smigelsky

DEFENSE
Defensive tackle: Bruce Smith
Defensive tackle: Scott Hill
Noseguard: Horacio Moronta
Drop end: Jesse Penn
Rush end: Robert Brown
Linebacker: Mike Johnson
Linebacker: Randy Cockrell
Cornerback: Roger Brown
Cornerback: Derek Carter
Strong safety: Sean Lucas
Free safety: Ashley Lee

Placekicker: Chris Kinzer

conditioning coach at Tech. The blow knocked out Beamer's right tooth. While students and players were swinging and punching each other, Whitten, Beamer and Tech team physician Dr. Duane Lagan were on their hands and knees looking for the tooth.

As rough as things were on Beamer physically in 1989, the season wasn't all bad. He secured his first winning season at Tech by beating North Carolina State, 25-23. The Hokies finished 6-4-1.

1990: RENEWED HOPE

Beamer's program appeared to have turned the corner in '89 and optimism was high for 1990. Seven or eight wins appeared possible and visions of bowl bids danced in optimistic fans' heads.

But the Hokies once again would face one of the most demanding schedules in the nation. After the season the NCAA ranked Tech's slate the seventh-toughest in the country. Tech still finished with a 6-5 mark and was competitive in every game.

SEMINOLES SCARED The Hokies almost pulled off the upset of the year on Sept. 29, 1990, in Tallahassee. Tech led No. 2 Florida State, 21-3, midway through the second quarter.

But two frustrating turnovers doomed the upset bid. Leading 28-25, Tech had the ball at its own 38-yard line after a Roger Garland interception. But FSU cornerback Terrell Buckley intercepted quarterback Will Furrer's

Cornerback Roger Brown was the star in Tech's 25-23 season-finale win at North Carolina State. He intercepted one pass and returned it 55 yards for a touchdown, then picked off another in the end zone to halt a scoring threat.

pass and made a dazzling 53-yard run into the end zone.

Trailing 32-28 with four minutes to play, the Hokies were driving for the winning score. On third-and-2 at the Florida State 33-yard line, Vaughn Hebron had already gotten the first down when Seminole linebacker Kirk Carruthers gave him a karate-chop across the arms. The ball bounced one time and right into the hands of cornerback Errol McCorvey, who never broke stride and sprinted 77 yards for a touchdown.

Talk about daggers in the heart. But the turnover was no fluke; Carruthers did exactly what he was trying to do.

"They had been running that pitch all night," Carruthers said. "I saw that Marvin Jones had the tackle, so I just concentrated on the ball. I located it and batted right at it."

FSU won, 39-28, but Tech proved it could play with any team in the nation.

TECH VS. TECH The Hokies were so close to having a monstrous season in '90. They lost four games after leading or holding a tie going into the final period. Against No. 7 Georgia Tech in Atlanta on Nov. 10, Tech led, 3-0, but gave up two field goals by Scott Sisson in the last 5:09. The Hokies played the game without their top two tailbacks, Vaughn Hebron and Ralph Brown.

"In *The Sporting News* a couple of weeks ago, I read

David Knachel's photograph on the cover of this Hokie Huddler said it all.

where [Virginia's] Shawn Moore was asked what team left on [UVa's] schedule he most feared," Sisson said after the game. "He said, 'Virginia Tech.' Now I know why."

OH, WHAT A NIGHT A win over the nationally-ranked Yellow Jackets might've sent Tech to its first bowl game under Beamer. Instead — as in 1983 — the Hokies pointed at their season finale with Virginia on Nov. 24 as that year's "bowl" game. And just like in '83, Tech came up a big winner.

Virginia came to Lane Stadium ranked No. 17 and was a six-point favorite. The largest crowd ever to see a football game in the state, 54,157, was on hand for the Saturday night game, televised nationally by ESPN.

Tech, wearing all-maroon outfits for the first time since 1984, also wore black shoes for the first time since 1977. Well, actually, they were white shoes spray-painted black.

"We were about the ugliest-looking team I've ever seen," Beamer said. "But our seniors wanted to do it. The way they played, I can't complain too much."

Senior linebacker Archie Hopkins gave the reason for

TECH JOINS THE BIG EAST

Since leaving the Southern Conference in the spring of 1965, Virginia Tech's football program operated as an independent for 26 seasons. Tech's big advantage as an independent was keeping all of the money it earned from television and bowl appearances.

But by the late 1980s those

advantages were gone. Conferences were cutting their own deals with television networks and bowls were creating tie-ins, not only with conference winners, but with second- and third-place finishers.

That created a problem for Tech Athletic Director Dave Braine, whose primary goal when he was brought to Blacksburg in 1987 was all-sports conference affiliation.

By the early 1990s the conference shuffles were on. Long-time independent Florida State joined the ACC. South Carolina joined the SEC.

Braine and Tech President James McComas lobbied their peers, trying to find a home for the Hokies' growing program.

Tech officially found that home on Feb. 5, 1991, when the Big East — known

he change. "It gave us a meaner image," he said.

It worked: Tech 38, Virginia 13. The win marked Beamer's first win over Virginia in four tries.

Virginia, which had already secured a Sugar Bowl bid, had been ranked No. 1 in the nation at one time and had also led the ACC for awhile. Alumnus/entrepreneur Dave Coby was ready for the occasion. By the final whistle he was hawking T-shirts that read: VIRGINIA, No. 1 in:

~~The Nation~~
~~The ACC~~
~~Virginia~~
Charlottesville

Monday's issue of *The Hokie Huddler* had an unprecedented cover: no words, just a David Knachel photograph of the scoreboard and goalposts buckling under the weight of joyous fans. Knachel, who has been snapping Tech sports since 1981, said it was the most popular photograph he's ever taken.

YOU WIN, YOU'RE IN One of the great advantages of Tech joining the Big East in 1991 was its bowl tie-ins. The league was a charter member of the bowl coalition and

From 1989-90, Frank Beamer posted two straight winning seasons against tough schedules. Half of his 22 opponents went to bowl games and seven teams were ranked in the Top 25 at the time of the game.

primarily as a basketball conference — added football at a special ceremony in Rhode Island. Tech joined Miami, Syracuse, Boston College, West Virginia, Rutgers, Temple, and Pitt as charter members of the Big East Football Conference.

It was a scene that would've made any Tech football fan proud. There was that maroon Virginia

One of Dave Braine's greatest achievements was getting Virginia Tech into the Big East for football. It helped turn the Hokies' program around.

Tech football helmet on a head table right next to the white helmet from Miami, the gold one from Boston College and the orange one from Syracuse.

This occurred at the stately, old-towne Providence Biltmore Hotel, the Big East's answer to the ACC's Sedgefield Inn.

"This is an historic day for Virginia Tech," Braine said. "For many years, Tech has operated at a disadvantage in football, competing as an independent. From the financial perspective and from the exposure perspective, we couldn't be in a better league."

Coach Frank Beamer was prophetic when he said, "Conference affiliation gives us the potential to be a Top-20 team on a consistent basis."

later the bowl alliance. That meant the league's winner would play in the Sugar, Orange or Fiesta bowl each year.

Additionally, the league arranged deals for three other Big East teams, meaning four of the eight teams would play in bowl games each year.

Remarkably, even before it played a single game, the league established its own syndicated television network that became the largest regional network in the country.

In 1994 the league signed a deal with CBS — which agreed to televise at least 12 Big East games per season — and ESPN, which would televise another 12. Both agreements would run through 2000 and ensure a Big East game on national television each week.

"The television exposure has been tremendous for us," Beamer said in 1995. "It used to be you had to explain a lot about Tech when you visited a recruit. Now, they know all about us and know all our players."

1991: HIGH HOPES

Enthusiasm was high with several publications, including *The Sporting News*, predicting a bowl bid for

Preseason publications predicted big things for quarterback Will Furrer in 1991.

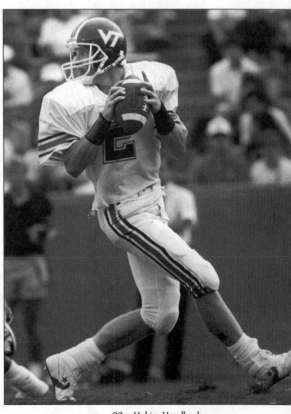

Tech, and almost all of the publications were raving about quarterback Will Furrer. "[Furrer is] most likely the top signal-caller in the new Big East," said *Football Digest*. "Now that is a story: A team from the Virginia mountains with the all-star quarterback in Miami's conference."

Tech was the consensus pick to finish third in the Big East behind Miami and Syracuse. *The Hokie Huddler* predicted a 7-4 record.

TOUGH ON THEMSELVES Working against Tech was a schedule that featured five straight road games against killer competition: North Carolina State, South Carolina, Oklahoma, West Virginia and Florida State. And the Hokies didn't give themselves any breaks, either.

A rehash of some excruciating losses revealed a litany of errors. Tech lost its season-opener, 7-0, at N.C. State after seven turnovers: five interceptions and two fumbles inside the Wolfpack 5-yard line. The Hokies fumbled three more times but managed to recover those.

The Hokies showcased a variety of gaffes in a 28-21 loss in Columbia on Sept. 21. They didn't have enough men on the line of scrimmage, negating one touchdown with 26 seconds left; Furrer overthrew a wide-open Steve Sanders in the end zone for another sure score; and Tech had three turnovers, including an interception at the goal line with seconds remaining.

Tech could've upset No. 6 Oklahoma on Sept. 28, but once again it was dogged by interceptions, fumbles and costly, inane penalties. Four such mistakes set up Sooner scores in a 27-17 loss before a crowd of 73,200 in Norman. A Hokie fumble at their own 36 set up one Sooner touchdown; another OU score was set up by a personal foul penalty when Tech hit a player who was clearly out of bounds. The Sooners' last touchdown was set up when the Hokies nailed an OU receiver in the back on an uncatchable ball. It didn't help that Tech started the second half with two straight interceptions, the latter returned for a score.

"There was nothing fancy about the Sooners' offense," Tech defensive coordinator Mike Clark said. "They basically run four or five plays. They beat you in January and February, in recruiting."

Against No. 1 Florida State, the Hokies outgained the Seminoles 420-323, but fell, 33-20, in the Citrus Bowl before a crowd of 58,991 on Oct. 12. Tech's record fell to 2-4.

Three interceptions and a fumble doomed the Hokies, even though it sacked Seminole quarterback Casey Weldon five times.

For the second straight year, FSU cornerback Terrell

Tech moved the 1991 Florida State game from Blacksburg to Orlando because of an $800,000 guarantee — a bigger payoff than many bowls.

HOKIES QUIZ

16. What was senior free safety William Yarborough's nickname?

Buckley returned a Furrer interception for a long touchdown. This time it was a 71-yarder. That gave the stellar Furrer the dubious distinction of throwing more touchdown passes to an opponent — Buckley — than to his own flanker, classmate Marcus Mickel, who caught just one in his career.

IT WAS THAT KIND OF YEAR The hard-luck 1991 season continued against No. 14 East Carolina on Nov. 16. Tech was coming off a three-game winning streak, with victories over Cincinnati (56-9), Louisville (41-13) and Akron (42-24). Things were looking good for a fourth straight win when the Hokies held a 14-7 lead and were threatening at the ECU 5-yard line. But reserve quarterback Rodd Wooten — pressed into action when Furrer's knee locked in warmups — was intercepted by Pirate safety Greg Grandison, who raced 95 yards untouched for a touchdown. East Carolina won, 24-17. Tech fell to 5-5.

The next week, without Furrer, an emotionally-drained Tech squad suffered one of its most embarrassing defeats ever: a 38-0 number to hated rival Virginia. The Hokies finished 5-6.

It wasn't an all gloom-and-doom season, however. In fact, the Hokies notched one of their most memorable wins ever in 1991.

THE LIGHTNING GAME A cloud of smoke exploded into the air. West Virginia's mascot had just fired his musket following tailback Adrian Murrell's 19-yard touchdown run, and WVU players were waving towels and whooping it up on the sidelines, exhorting their rain-soaked home-coming fans. The Mountaineer Field lights flickered on.

Behind backup quarterback Chris Gray, West Virginia had charged back to within six of Virginia Tech, 20-14, on the last play of the third quarter.

A bolt of lightning flashed across the sky. Things looked ominous, and not just for the Hokies.

That's when, at 2:36 p.m. on Oct. 5, 1991, the officials sent both teams to their locker rooms. Play was temporarily suspended.

"In 33 years of coaching," WVU coach Don Nehlen said, "I've never seen a game delayed."

"I thought that delay may have come at a good time," Tech coach Frank Beamer would say later. "They had a lot of momentum going for them."

The press box was buzzing during the break. Reporters converged on Big East Commissioner Mike Tranghese, on hand to see Virginia Tech live. After all, this was the Hokies' first game against an official Big East opponent.

"We'll finish the game," he said, "but we just can't

take any chances."

In Tech's locker room, tailback Tony Kennedy rubbed ointment on his sore hamstring. "It was a battle to keep it from tightening up," he said.

Other Hokie players took their pads off while the coaching staff formulated their fourth-quarter plan. West Virginia had started the game with an option attack under Darren Studstill. But when that failed, it switched to a passing and straight-ahead running plan with Gray. Tech had to adjust.

"We're in Morgantown and we have the lead," Beamer told his players. "Now it's time for us to win the ballgame."

The rain stopped at 3:06 p.m. After the delay, neither team could score. But the Mountaineers tried. They really did.

A miracle catch by Mike Beasley on fourth down kept their late drive alive. Gray's pass went off cornerback John Granby's hands and Beasley alertly clamped onto it as he fell backward out of bounds at the Tech 25-yard line.

Another completion and a penalty put the ball on Tech's 5-yard line with 1:20 left.

"I just grabbed Eugene's [offensive tackle Chung] hand and held on," said quarterback Will Furrer, who could only watch, helplessly, on the sideline. "I saw it worked for [former Hokie defensive back] Roger Brown

James Hargrove helped save the day against WVU in '91.

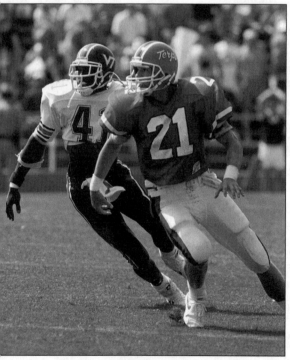

Damien Russell was a key member of "the Dark Zone."

in the Super Bowl."

It worked for Furrer, too. On third down from the one-yard line, Tech stopped WVU fullback Rod Woodard. Then, on fourth down with just 20 seconds left, Tech end James Hargrove forced and recovered a Gray fumble. It was Tech's first game-winning goal line stand since a 23-16 win at Auburn in 1975. The Hokies celebrated shamelessly and were flagged for unsportsmanlike

DESPITE HANDICAP, RYAN DID FINE

From Chris Kinzer to Mickey Thomas to Ryan Williams, Virginia Tech had a straight-on style kicker from 1985-1994.

Kinzer and Thomas had a choice. Williams didn't. He lost half of his right foot in an accident when he was 5 years old.

It was Sept. 10, 1977. The family's eldest son, Rich, was aboard a riding lawn mower trimming the grass alongside the house; as he backed up, Ryan ran around the corner. The mower blade clipped his right foot.

The family rushed him to the hospital; when the doctor looked at Ryan's mangled foot, he decided to amputate.

"Even after the operation, I wasn't sure what had happened," Williams said. "The doctor had kept my foot covered while I was in the hospital. After a couple of weeks they showed it to me. I looked down and there were no toes; just stitches and iodine stains. It was a shock."

At first he used a leather filler to fit in the empty section of his shoe, but he eventually tossed it. His grandfather fashioned him a half-shoe, which he began wearing in the eighth grade. "I had nothing to hide," he said.

Williams lettered in football, basketball and lacrosse at Nansemond-Suffolk Academy. On Fork Union Military Academy's undergraduate team, he concentrated on placekicking and earned all-league and All-Central Virginia honors, making 11 of 15 field goal attempts. There was never any doubt, however, where he was going to college. "Everybody in my family is a Hokie," he said.

With his half-shoe and booming leg, naturally there were the comparisons to Tom Dempsey, born with half a foot, who holds the record for the longest field goal in NFL history (63 yards). In fact, Williams' shoe was based on Dempsey's design. "I saw the one Dempsey used on display at the Pro Football Hall of Fame," said former Washington Redskins placekicker Mark Moseley, the NFL's MVP in 1982. "I drew up a picture of it and sent it to his mother, and she sent it to a certified prosthetist."

Moseley served as a mentor to Williams. "If I have any problems with my kicking, I can call him any time of day and he'll give me some kind of answer to correct it," Williams said.

Williams' first chance to show his stuff came on Sept. 28, 1991, against sixth-ranked Oklahoma in Norman. He nailed a 50-yarder for his first collegiate kick.

It would always be easy for Williams to remember the length of that one. It was the same as his conduct. It didn't matter; the ball was already at the one-yard line. Furrer kept it and ran out the clock, and Tech had an unprecedented third straight win over West Virginia.

Kennedy led all rushers with 104 yards, and the Hokies took advantage of five WVU turnovers including interceptions by Tyronne Drakeford, DeWayne Knight, and West Virginia native Marcus McClung.

ersey number.

He went on to convert 39 of 57 field goals and 137 of 147 extra points for a school-record career total of 254 points.

In 1996, *Athlon Sports Annual* voted Williams' career as the Greatest Performance to Overcome Obstacles in college football history.

Ryan Williams is Virginia Tech's career scoring leader.

THE DARK ZONE Virginia Tech's 1991 defensive backfield of John Granby, Greg Lassiter, Tyronne Drakeford, Damien Russell and Kirk Alexander was a talented group; Drakeford is still with the San Francisco 49ers, while Russell and Granby had short NFL stints.

They felt like they needed a nickname. "We all sat down at the end of last season, and with all the guys coming back we figured we needed something," Russell said. "We started spitting out names and 'the Dark Zone' stuck.

"You step into 'the Dark Zone,' " he explained, "and it's 'lights out.' "

Defensive backfield coach Keith Jones wasn't overly enthusiastic about the moniker. "I don't have a problem with it," he said, "as long as they back it up."

One day in practice Tech split end Bo Campbell caught a long pass. "I must have had a flashlight," he said, ribbing Russell and company. That wasn't even the best of the jabs thrown at the group by their good-natured offensive teammates. To wit:

"You guys are more like 'the Score Zone!' "

" 'The Dark Zone?' That's the area of the field you go through before the end zone!"

THE YEAR FROM HELL The bitter disappointment of 1991 seemed to carry over into the 1992 season, one of the most frustrating in school history. It wasn't like back in 1950, when the Hokies were just plain awful. This club had talent; most of the same players would lead Tech to the 1993 Independence Bowl. Many observers thought the Hokies could go 6-5.

But nothing seemed to go right, and Tech lost game after game in excruciating fashion.

Tech finished the year 2-8-1 and had just one Division I-A win all season, beating 1-10 Temple. Its defense allowed 17 touchdown passes, most in school history.

Fiery Phil Elmassian added a new dimension to Tech's football program.

New coaches on Beamer's staff for 1993 included Phil Elmassian, who took over as defensive coordinator; offensive line coach J.B. Grimes; tight ends coach Bryan Stinespring; and defensive ends coach Rod Sharpless. Beamer switched Terry Strock from defense to handle Tech's receivers. And he handed the offensive coordinator duties to quarterbacks coach Rickey Bustle.

In addition to the new faces, Beamer implemented fresh perspectives on both offense and defense. He scrapped the wide-tackle six in favor of a 4-3-4 defensive alignment, choosing to emphasize a faster, attacking unit.

Rickey Bustle took over as offensive coordinator in 1993.

Offensively, he now had a much more efficient logistical system. Before, Steve Marshall — who left the Hokie staff to join Tennessee — doubled as offensive coordinator and line coach. It was probably a bit much

Cornerback Tyronne Drakeford earned first team All-Big East honors in 1992.

to expect Marshall to call the right plays and coach five men during a game. With Bustle calling the plays, Tech had an extension of the quarterback. It made good sense.

1993: GLORY DAYS

Nobody expected much from the Hokies in 1993. Several publications predicted 3-8 or 4-7 records. *The Hokie Huddler* predicted a 5-6 mark. The Big East media picked Tech to finish sixth in the league.

Newspapers criticized Beamer's 1992 team as being undisciplined, and they had a point: Tech was penalized 88 times for 755 yards that season.

Tech's 2-0 start in 1993 was its best since 1981.

The Hokies' lack of mettle changed in '93, though. Beamer took fewer players on road trips. He outlawed hats in meeting rooms. He emphasized fundamentals. And he began practicing in full pads on Monday, previously a non-contact day.

The contact practices became more intense, with first-

A panel of Football News *prognosticators picked Pitt to win by 17, 10, 7 and 6 points. One panelist picked the Hokies to win by 2. The consensus pick: Pitt by 12.*

teamers going against first-teamers. "A lot of guys were moaning about it," defensive tackle J.C. Price said. "But the coaches kept telling us there was a reason they were making it so hard. And it paid off. We've suffered and sweated together; we've put too much work in not to try our best in games."

FINDING THE RIGHT FIT AT PITT Although Tech dispatched Bowling Green in perfunctory style, 33-16, in the home-opener Sept. 4, the "new" era under Beamer really began the following Saturday night in Pittsburgh.

The Panthers were coming off a 14-10 upset at Southern Mississippi and were thought to be much improved. But Tech gained a school-record 500 yards on the ground en route to a 63-21 win.

Tech's offense sputtered at No. 3 Miami in a 21-2 loss

Split end Antonio Freeman had some big games for the Hokies in 1993. He caught five passes for 122 yards and a score against Maryland, then set a Big East single-game mark with 194 yards receiving against Temple.

on Sept. 18, but rebounded the following week with a 55-28 win over Maryland in rainy Blacksburg. That game set Lane Stadium records for highest combined score (83 points); highest combined total offense (1,290 yards); most total offense by Tech (641 yards); most touchdown passes by an individual (four by Maurice DeShazo).

Then Tech's offense struggled again, this time at No. 22 West Virginia in a 14-13 loss.

SHOTGUN START To help jump start its struggling offense, Tech — at the time 3-2 —installed a shotgun formation with four wideouts in the off-week preceding the Oct. 16 Temple game (there was talk of changing Tech's sports newsletter name to *The Hokie No-Huddler*). The result: a 55-7 victory, with DeShazo passing for a career-high 325 yards. "It does the same things for us that it does for Charlie Ward at Florida State," Beamer said. "They let him do his thing and we want Maurice to do his."

RANKED AGAIN AT LAST After a 49-42 win over Rutgers and a 31-12 victory over East Carolina, Tech was 6-2 and

Tech's 55-7 win over Temple in '93 marked its first Big East league victory in Lane Stadium.

Tech touted Maurice DeShazo as a Heisman Trophy candidate after his dazzling '93 campaign: 129-for-230 passing for 2,080 yards and 22 touchdown passes.

Jim Pyne was more than just fine for Tech. He was the school's first unanimous All-American. On Nov. 1, 1993, Sports Illustrated ran a story on the center titled "Born To Block."

broke into the Associated Press poll for the first time since 1986. The Hokies were also ranked in the USA Today/CNN Coaches' Poll for the second straight week, which hadn't happened since 1954.

Tech's 45-24 win over Syracuse in '93 broke the Hokies' three-game losing streak to the Orangemen.

Tech then met Boston College for the first time ever, losing, 48-34. Beamer brought in former Tech coach Jerry Claiborne to give an inspirational speech before the Syracuse game. It was a great move, as the Hokies bounced back with a 45-24 win.

When the game was over, seniors Chris Barry, John Burke and Joe Swarm drenched Beamer with water.

Following the game, Independence Bowl Chairman Mike McCarthy extended Tech, with a 7-3 record, its first bowl invitation since 1986.

TECH GETS AN 'A' FOR WIN OVER UVA With a bowl bid in hand, Virginia Tech traveled to Charlottesville playing for pride and looking to break a losing streak. The Hokies had not won in Scott Stadium since 1985.

Tech's 1993 20-17 win over Virginia was its first over a ranked team on the road since 1989.

They prevailed with a 20-17 win over No. 23 Virginia. Many fans remember tackle Jeff Holland's eight-yard

Tailback Dwayne Thomas averaged 5.3 yards per carry in 1993, gaining 1,130 yards and scoring 11 touchdowns, to becomeTech's first 1,000-yard rusher since 1986.

fumble return for a score in the second quarter. But the play of the game came in the third quarter, with Tech leading, 17-10, and Virginia inside the Hokies' 10-yard line. Tech stuffed Jerrod Washington on a third-down option play at the 7-yard line, setting up a UVa field goal. But linebacker George DelRicco was flagged for unsportsmanlike conduct for taunting kicker Kyle Kirkeide, bringing up a fourth-and-1 situation from the Tech 3-yard line. Coach George Welsh decided to go for it, but DelRicco and teammate Torrian Gray swallowed up Washington for no gain. Instead of at least three points, the Wahoos had nothing.

UVa was tough at home that year, too. The Wahoos had beaten No. 13 North Carolina in Scott Stadium earlier the same season.

Jeff Holland became the first Tech defensive lineman to score a touchdown since 1970.

HUSTLING AND BUSTLE-ING Rickey Bustle's touch as offensive coordinator in '93 was almost magical. Tech set a single-season mark for total offense with 4,885 yards, breaking the old record of 4,534 set in 1983. The team was the first in school history to gain more than 2,200 yards both rushing and passing. Of course, the Hokies stayed healthy on offense; nine players played every game, while the other two missed just one game each. Tech also scored a school-record 400 points.

FANS GOT THE FEVER Ten years earlier, Tech had taken just 1,855 fans to the 1984 Independence Bowl. This time 6,500 fans went.

J.C. Price loved playing in a bowl, but he couldn't get a burger when he wanted one.

Former Pittsburgh Steeler great Terry Bradshaw was a featured speaker at the 1993 Independence Bowl.

The Hokies were three-point favorites over Indiana in the Independence Bowl.

But while more fans were making the trip to Shreveport, the Hokie team was taking fewer players. Only the ones who might see action made the trip; Tech took 65 players; Indiana took 109.

INDEPENDENCE BOWL Virginia Governor (and former Cavalier football player) George Allen was on hand for Tech's first bowl game since 1986, wearing a Hokie cap and orange-and-maroon-striped tie, cheering for Tech.

Two big plays at the end of the first half turned the game around. With :23 left before intermission,

In one of the most memorable plays in school history, Antonio Banks returned a blocked punt 80 yards for a touchdown. The two quick scores effectively sealed the Independence Bowl trophy for the Hokies.

Lawrence Lewis picked up a fumble and ran 20 yards for a score. As uncommon as that score was, it couldn't compare to what was to happen next.

Indiana returned the ensuing kickoff to the Tech 42-yard line; then quarterback John Paci found Eddie Baety near — but inside — the left sideline for nine yards. The Hokies thought time had expired and trotted off the field. IU coach Bill Mallory argued that his team called a time-out with one second left. The officials concurred and waved Tech back.

Maurice DeShazo was named Outstanding Offensive Player of the '93 Independence Bowl and Antonio Banks was named Outstanding Defensive Player.

"You blew it!" Coach Frank Beamer shouted. Then he turned to his field goal defense team. "Make them pay for that!" he said.

The ball was snapped, and Tech tackle Jeff Holland pushed through the center of the line, tipping Bill Manolopolous' 51-yard try. The ball caromed into the air, and the Hokies' Antonio Banks settled under it at the Tech 20-yard line.

"It was a freak play," Banks said. "You're supposed to get away from the ball in that situation, but it came in so high and it looked so good, I just had to go for it."

Banks started to his right, then reversed his direction as a wall of blockers formed. At about the 15-yard line, his main escort, Torrian Gray, took care of IU's Chris Dyer and allowed Banks to strut into the end zone untouched.

"After we scored the touchdown, I looked at the officials and said, 'Nice call!' " Beamer said. "I guess those guys knew what they were doing."

Mallory was wishing he had lost the argument. "That

Steve Sanders celebrated with Hokie fans after the Indy Bowl victory.

play really cut our throats," he said. "That was the last thing in the world we wanted to see happen."

Indiana's players were reeling. "Shocking," said Hoosier defensive end Hurvin McCormack. "Some freaky things happened out there. I've never seen anything like it before."

Tech beat the Hoosiers, 45-20, setting an Independence Bowl record for most points by one team.

1994: THE NEXT LEVEL

Gary Tranquill became Tech's third different offensive coordinator in three years.

The future of Tech football appeared bright. On the two-deep roster for the 1993 squad that went 9-3, there were 12 sophomores, nine redshirt freshmen and five true freshmen. The Hokies had finished the season ranked No. 22 in the AP poll and No. 20 in the coaches' poll.

Naturally, big things were expected in 1994. Tech was ranked as high as No. 17 and nearly everyone had the Hokies in the Top 25. The Big East media predicted a second-place league finish.

If the Hokies were going to duplicate their terrific offensive output of a year ago, however, they were going to do it without maestro Rickey Bustle, who left to become offensive coordinator at South Carolina. Tech hired Gary Tranquill from the Cleveland Browns to replace him.

FAST START After an easy 34-7 season-opening win over Arkansas State on Sept. 3, the Hokies sweated out a 24-14 victory over Southern Mississippi in Hattiesburg

Bryan Still's 41-yard touchdown catch against Southern Miss was one of the game's big plays.

on Sept. 10 to go 2-0. Tech lost four fumbles and had two passes intercepted as the Golden Eagles took a 14-0 lead. But Tech's defense was stellar, holding Southern Mississippi to just 144 total yards. Quarterback Maurice DeShazo's 41-yard touchdown pass to Bryan Still in the fourth quarter gave Tech its first lead.

The Hokies had a breakthrough 12-7 win at Boston College on Sept. 17. It marked Tech's first road victory over an upper-echelon Big East team and improved the team's record to 3-0.

Even though the Hokies' offense struggled again, their defense — ranked third nationally — was superb. The big play: a Torrian Gray 66-yard interception return for a score.

"In all my years of coaching, I've never seen a bunch like this," said defensive coordinator Phil Elmassian, one not prone to gushing. "They've only had two bad practices since the Independence Bowl."

Atle Larsen became the first soccer-style kicker to convert a field goal for Tech since Tom Taricani in 1985.

DELIVERING Beamer handed out pizzas to students waiting in line for West Virginia tickets and he delivered in a different way when his No. 14 Hokies waxed WVU, 34-6, in a Thursday night, Sept. 22 ESPN telecast. "That's the hardest we've been hit this year," Mountaineer wide receiver Zach Abraham said.

The win marked Tech's 100th in Lane Stadium.

Quarterback Maurice DeShazo threw three interceptions, but the Hokie defense racked up eight sacks. Tech's 28-point margin of victory was its largest against WVU since the opening game of the series in

ESPN TV cameras were part of a packed house for the 1994 Tech-WVU Thursday night game.

Linebacker George DelRicco was the Hokie ringleader against WVU with 14 tackles, a sack, two quarterback hurries, a pass broken up and two forced fumbles. He was named Big East Co-Defensive Player of the Week.

Tech issued 284 press credentials to the 1994 Tech-West Virginia game — 75 to ESPN. Mike Patrick and Mike Gottfried were in the booth, with Dr. Jerry Punch on the sidelines.

1912. The Mountaineers failed to score a touchdown against the Hokies for the first time since 1978.

SLOWED AT SYRACUSE The Hokies' 4-0 roll took a temporary halt at No. 22 Syracuse in a game televised regionally by ABC that marked Tech's first network appearance in 11 years.

Ranked No. 10 in the coaches' poll, the Hokies were 5 ½-point favorites. Tech entered the game ranked No. 1 nationally in pass defense and No. 2 in total defense. But its crew tired in the fourth quarter and the Orangemen won, 28-20.

Then Tech got back on track with three straight wins against Temple (41-13), Liberty Bowl-bound East Carolina (27-20) and Pittsburgh (45-7). The win over Pitt pushed Tech to No. 10 in the coaches' poll and a

The key play of Tech's 27-20 win over ECU was a 60-yard fumble return for a touchdown by Hokie defensive end Lawrence Lewis.

best-ever No. 13-ranking in the AP. Tech's 7-1 start was its best since 1967.

ORANGE BLUES Tech dropped to 7-2 the next week after a 24-3 defeat at No. 4 Miami in a game televised by ABC at the Orange Bowl. And after an open week, Tech beat Rutgers, 41-34, at home.

Unfortunately Tech lost linebacker Ken Brown with a strained hamstring on the last play of the first half against RU. Without him in the lineup, Rutgers scored 21 second-half points. Tech held on to win, but missed him badly the following week against Virginia. Tech moved Brandon Semones to backer and moved freshman Tony Morrison to Semones' whip spot.

Scouts from the Fiesta, Gator, Carquest, Peach and Independence bowls were on hand for the battle of two nationally-ranked state rivals. Tech was No. 11 in the coaches' poll and No. 14 in the AP; Virginia was 14 and 16, respectively. The Hokies were one-point favorites.

But Tech turned it over eight times — five

Outside linebacker Brandon Semones was named Big East Defensive Player of the Week after registering 15 tackles, three sacks, two forced fumbles, a quarterback pressure and a pass broken up against Pitt in '94.

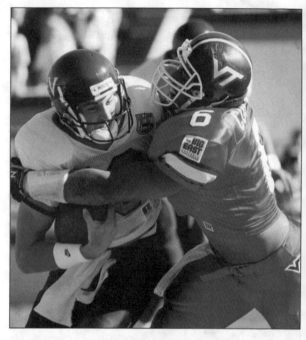

After a less-than-spectacular outing against Virginia, Frank Beamer decided to shelve Tech's all-orange uniforms.

interceptions and three fumbles — in a 42-23 loss on Nov. 19. UVa had the ball 40 minutes, Tech had it 20.

BIGGEST BOWL EVER The Hokies finished 8-3 and accepted a Gator Bowl bid — the most lucrative postseason offer in school history at $1.5 million. Ironically, Syracuse handed Tech one loss, yet did not receive a bowl bid. Virginia also beat the Hokies but went to the lesser Independence Bowl.

Over 19,000 Hokie fans traveled to Gainesville for the 1994 Gator Bowl.

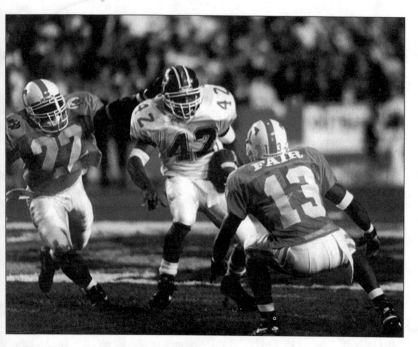

GATOR BOWL Tech entered the Gator Bowl ranked 15th in the coaches' poll and 17th in the AP. Even so, unranked Tennessee was a seven-point favorite.

The Volunteers, an SEC power playing in an SEC stadium — Ben Hill Griffin Stadium at Florida Field — intercepted DeShazo on the game's second play. Tech never seemed to recover from that disappointment in a 45-23 loss.

Wrote *The Hokie Huddler*: "Virginia Tech got a taste of the Southeastern Conference Dec. 30 in Gainesville, Fla. But instead of caviar and champagne, it tasted more like limburger cheese coated in cough medicine."

Renovations to Jacksonville's Gator Bowl had forced the game to be played in Gainesville.

One bright spot was tailback Dwayne Thomas, who gained 102 yards on 19 carries and scored a touchdown.

UT's Peyton Manning completed 12 of 19 passes for 189 yards and a score. Jim Druckenmiller gave a hint of what was to come when he completed six of eight passes for 97 yards and a score.

Dwayne Thomas was a rare bright spot for Tech in the Gator Bowl.

The Hokies finished No. 24 in the coaches' and No. 26 in the Associated Press polls after the 1994 season.

1995
The Dream Season

Before the season started, William Yarborough told fans gathered at a rally that there wouldn't be "that many" losses in 1995.

Virginia Tech's greatest football season seemed even sweeter in that a string of setbacks preceded it. There was the Gator Bowl embarrassment, a 45-23 loss to Tennessee. Then the Hokies signed a recruiting class most "experts" rated as just average. Defensive coordinator Phil Elmassian left to join the University of Washington's staff, saying he wanted to "compete for the national championship." Beamer named Bud Foster and Rod Sharpless as co-defensive coordinators, and some wondered how such an arrangement would work. There was little defensive depth at linebacker and the secondary. And the Hokies didn't have a quarterback with starting experience.

But 17 starters returned, including 10 of 11 defensive starters. And back, too, was offensive coordinator Rickey Bustle, returning from South Carolina.

ESPNet's Sportszone picked Tech No. 10; *Athlon*, No. 15; *Lindy's*, No. 18; Associated Press, No. 25. *The Sporting News* refused to believe, picking the Hokies No. 37.

The Hokie Huddler predicted an 8-3 season and either a Gator or Carquest bowl bid.

The 6-foot-4, 222-pound Jim Druckenmiller gave those in the know a glimpse of what was in store that

Jim Druckenmiller kicked off a stellar junior season by capturing Tech's offseason Iron Man championship.

summer when he won the off-season Iron Man competition. "I know two things to be true in this world," said Tech assistant weightlifting coach Scott Bennett. "A hundred pounds of flour makes an awfully big biscuit, and Druckenmiller is one strong man."

SEPTEMBER 14:
BOSTON COLLEGE 20, TECH 14

Virginia Tech's greatest season ever began inauspiciously.

Boston College — taking advantage of numerous Tech season-opening mistakes — prevailed, 20-14, in a game televised by ESPN (Mike Patrick, Mike Gottfried and Dr. Jerry Punch) from Blacksburg.

Despite the loss, the Hokies' quarterbacking fears were assuaged. Working out of a no-huddle offense, Druckenmiller completed 21 of 42 passes for 296 yards, a record for a Tech quarterback making his collegiate starting debut. "Their quarterback is going to be a force," said BC coach Dan Henning, a man who is known for his

With the Hokies' 38-16 win over Temple, Frank Beamer evened his Virginia Tech coaching record at 49-49-2. Ironically, he was 49 years old at the time.

Jim Druckenmiller had a spectacular starting debut.

17. What former Hokie has started more consecutive football games than anybody in school history?

work with signal-callers. "He was poised and he knew what he wanted to do."

Flanker Bryan Still caught three passes for 105 yards before separating his shoulder. Most of those yards came on a beautiful play where he took a short swing pass and — in stride — completely faked out a BC defender and sped 80 yards for a score.

Most Tech fans, however, were talking about the passes that were not caught. Hokie receivers bobbled no fewer than six tosses. Even more galling was the fact that Tech outgained BC by the length of a football field (418-318) — yet lost.

SEPTEMBER 16:
CINCINNATI 16, TECH 0

The Bearcats upset the Hokies in Blacksburg on a muddy Worsham Field.

Tech gained just 239 net yards, and fans began to question the merits of the no-huddle. Hokie receivers were dropping balls at an alarming rate. Tight end Bryan Jennings was getting few looks. And remember, at this point Tech had lost five of its last six games — the one victory was a squeaker at home over Rutgers — and had dropped three in a row at home dating back to 1994.

With an 0-2 start and No. 17 Miami coming to town, things didn't look good for the Hokies, who had never beaten the Hurricanes.

SEPTEMBER 23:
TECH 13, MIAMI 7

Instead of pointing fingers, the Hokies — who were 9 ½-point underdogs — rallied together.

And they went back to running the football. A year

Tech's defensive front was the difference in its 13-7 win over Miami.

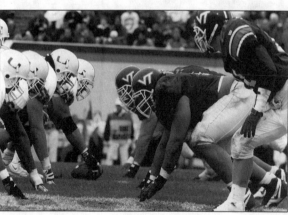

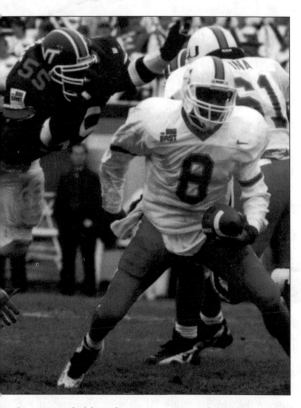

Flying linebacker Myron Newsome typified Tech's tenacity against the vaunted Hurricanes.

earlier Miami held Tech to minus 14 yards rushing. But not this year. The Hokies rushed on their first nine plays and 24 of 33 plays in the first half. Overall they ran on 49 of 65 plays, gaining 300 yards on the ground.

Tailback Dwayne Thomas had 165 yards on 25 carries as Tech won one of the most important games in school history. Without this win, the Big East Championship and Sugar Bowl bid would not have been possible.

Defensively, the Hokies were superb. Tackle J.C. Price had one of the greatest games in school history with nine

The Hokies' upset of the Hurricanes set off a wild celebration in Lane Stadium.

tackles and four sacks and was named Big East Defensive Player of the Week.

The Hokies could've clobbered the 'Canes, but they missed three field goals, had a fourth blocked and dropped a touchdown pass.

The 38-16 win over Temple was Tech's eighth straight, its longest winning streak since — ahem — 1905.

As it was, the game came down to the final 17 seconds, when freshman cornerback Loren Johnson knocked away a pass intended for Yatil Green at the Tech 5-yard line. This was the same Yatil Green who caught a 25-yard desperation pass just before halftime a year earlier in Tech's loss at the Orange Bowl. There was contact, but no flag. Johnson and fellow freshman Pierson Prioleau did a great job replacing Antonio Banks, who was out with a knee injury.

"When we lost to Cincinnati last week, it was the lowest point of my career," said running backs coach Billy Hite, who has been a Tech assistant for 18 seasons.

THIS PRICE WAS RIGHT

Senior defensive tackle J.C. Price was straight out of NFL Films: a down-and-dirty throwback with the blood-and-guts toughness of a player from the 1950s. He'd be right at home wearing a single-bar facemask and playing on the frozen tundra of Lambeau Field.

"He reminds me of one of those old-time football guys," Coach Frank Beamer said. "But even though he's a throwback in his mannerisms, he's a contemporary player in that he's big [6-3, 285] and nifty. He's one of the top defensive linemen ever to play at Virginia Tech."

Price came to Virginia Tech with a high school nickname, "Ogre," a scruffy goatee and a haircut that was shaved on the sides. "He looks like a hellraiser," one athletic department employee offered upon seeing Price's file photo.

"The first day he arrived on campus he had that goatee and wild hair," said assistant coach Billy Hite, who recruited Price. "Coach Beamer saw him and gave me a look. He raised his eyebrows and

said to me, 'Billy, that kid better be a player.'"

Price lived up to his hell-raising image as a freshman. "Let's see," he told *Roanoke Times* sportswriter Randy King. "My day would go like this: I'd wake up about noon, eat lunch, play Sega, go to practice, come home, play Sega, drink beer, stay up until about 6 o'clock in the morning, go to sleep and start all over again."

Price never went to class or did any homework. He finished his first semester with three Fs and a D. His parents taped the report card to the family television during Christmas. His failures were there for everybody to see over the holidays. "It was awfully humbling," Price said.

With help from his parents and coaches, he began to turn things around, and by his junior year he had earned a 2.9 grade point average.

As his grades improved, so did his game. One of Price's most amazing plays came his senior year against Miami when he tackled swift Hurricane wide receiver

"And now, I can honestly say this is the biggest win I've ever been a part of."

SHUT UP, ALREADY The Hokies' win was sweet for senior offensive guard Chris Malone, who grew up hating Miami's program. "I didn't like all that taunting and showboating," he said. "I'm more of a blue-collar guy. I always wanted to beat the crap out of them."

Tech's game-long lead quieted most of the trash-talking. "Now they're not as loquacious as they used to be," he said. A reporter asked him how to spell "loquacious," and Malone spelled it out correctly. "I am a true student-athlete," he said with a smile.

Chris Malone: quite the speller.

By the end of the season, Malone had secured his place in Hokie history when he started a Tech record 47 games: all 11 regular season games for four years and three bowl games.

Jammi German — after a 37-yard completion. Price didn't so much use his speed, although he ran the 40 in under five seconds; it was more his tenacity. Most linemen rushing the passer would've given up on the play after the pass was thrown, but not Price. He doesn't think that way. German had caught the ball and cut across the field and Price followed him. "I was going to follow their guys all over the field," Price said. "I was going to follow them into the bathroom if I had to."

J.C. Price: a blood-and-guts throwback.

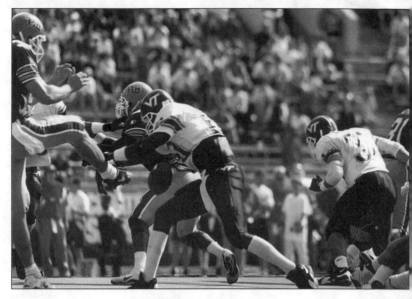

Freshman Angelo Harrison blocked two punts at Pitt.

Flanker Bryan Still became the first Tech player ever to be on the receiving end of two passes of 80 yards or more. He went 80 yards for a score against Boston College then latched onto an 85-yard bomb against Pitt.

SEPTEMBER 30:
TECH 26, PITTSBURGH 16

Wearing stripeless maroon pants for the first time in the modern era, Tech trailed 9-0 at halftime in Pittsburgh. But freshman Angelo Harrison blocked two punts in the second half, setting up 10 Hokie points. That gave him three blocked punts in two games and earned him notice on ESPN.

Druckenmiller had two big fourth-quarter bombs to set up scores. He connected with Jermaine Holmes for a 73-yard scoring pass, then hit Still for 85 yards, setting up a field goal.

Panther tailback Billy West had gained 113 yards on 23 carries, but the Hokies knocked him out with a broken ankle with 6:19 left in the third quarter.

Tech's win marked its best comeback since 1990.

OCTOBER 7:
TECH 14, NAVY 0

The Hokies dispatched Navy as junior defensive end Cornell Brown had 16 tackles. Many fans, however, might forget one of the biggest plays of the game. The Hokies were going nowhere but backward on their fourth series of the game. With fourth-and-15, John I. Thomas came in to punt from his own 24-yard line.

"The ball slipped through my hands and hit my chest," Thomas said. "I felt [Navy's] pressure coming

THE LUNCH PAIL

Tech co-defensive coordinator Rod Sharpless' mother-in-law found Tech's now-famous lunch pail in Mercerville, N.J., where it had belonged to a coal miner. "It's a symbol of our defense," Tech co-defensive coordinator Bud Foster said. "We're blue-collar guys who bring their lunch to work every day. The pail goes with us everywhere we go: practice, team meetings, the bus, the plane, the hotel."

Tech's top defensive player of the week was responsible for the pail.

Cornell Brown proudly displays the Lunch Pail, which symbolized Tech's blue-collar work ethic.

from my left, so I stepped to my right. That way they'd have to run through me to get to the ball."

Thomas still wasn't out of trouble. If he had kicked the ball conventionally, Navy might still have blocked it. Instead he side-legged it and somehow got it away before the Midshipmen arrived to nail him.

Since Navy didn't get a piece of the ball, officials called roughing the kicker, giving the Hokies new life at their 39-yard line. Six plays later Druckenmiller found Jermaine Holmes for a 16-yard touchdown.

That would be the game's only score until Dwayne Thomas danced down the left sideline for a 28-yard touchdown with 1:55 left.

The Big East Football Conference named Thomas its Special Teams Player of the Week after he averaged 42.7 yards per punt.

But he could've won the award on the one kick that didn't count.

Tech had Wallenda-like balance in its 31-7 win over Syracuse in 1995: 224 yards passing and 224 yards rushing.

OCTOBER 14:
TECH 77, AKRON 27

Tech's struggling offense exploded for a modern-era record 77 points in a homecoming game against the Zips in Blacksburg. The Hokies had scored just 67 points in five previous games.

Their 11 touchdowns and eight rushing scores set school records and marked Tech's largest margin of victory since 1969. The teams combined for a Lane

Tech's five defensive touchdowns in 1995 set a school record. The previous high of four was recorded in both 1967 and 1968, when Frank Beamer was a cornerback.

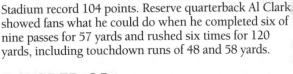

Against Akron, backup Al Clark got a rare chance to strut his stuff. His 58-yard touchdown run was the longest for a Tech quarterback since 1977.

Stadium record 104 points. Reserve quarterback Al Clark showed fans what he could do when he completed six of nine passes for 57 yards and rushed six times for 120 yards, including touchdown runs of 48 and 58 yards.

OCTOBER 21:
TECH 45, RUTGERS 17

Offensive coordinator Rickey Bustle missed the first half because of a painful kidney stone, but it didn't matter.

By the time he arrived at Rutgers Stadium, Tech already had the game well in hand. Then its defense tallied two late scores. First Hank Coleman returned a fumble 51 yards to make it 38-17. Then there was "Voice of the Hokies" Bill Roth's famous "Double Nickels" call of No. 55, Myron Newsome, returning an interception 71 yards for a score. The return was Tech's longest interception return for a score since Randy Cockrell's 90-yard return in 1990. Newsome had 10 tackles, a sack and broke up a pass as the Big East named him Defensive Player of the Week. Both *Sports Illustrated* and *The Sporting News* named him National Defensive Player of the Week.

Myron Newsome was Sports Illustrated's National Defensive Player of the Week for his work at Rutgers.

OCTOBER 29:
TECH 27, WEST VIRGINIA 0

Tech whipped West Virginia at Morgantown in a series that had become increasingly lopsided. The Hokies had beaten the Mountaineers by a combined score of 61-6 the last two years and tallied an astounding 16 sacks.

Cornell Brown was the Big East Defensive Player of the Week with 12 tackles and three sacks. "Cornell was

FEUDIN' IN BLUEFIELD

While the University of Virginia has always been the biggest rival for most Virginia Tech fans, West Virginia is close behind — particularly for fans in southwest Virginia. In no place is the rivalry greater than in Bluefield, a town that sits on the Virginia/West Virginia state line.

The sign on Route 460 simply says "Welcome to the Bluefields," and you're never really sure which state you're in when you visit this hotbed of sports enthusiasm. And you're not sure if the locals are Hokie or Mountaineer fans.

Each year at the Hokie Club spring dinner, a representative from the Mountaineer Athletic Club must attend to accept either the grief of a WVU football loss or brag about a win over the Hokies. Similarly, the Hokie Club president must attend the WVU meeting later in the spring. The loser each year receives a trophy — in the shape of the backside of a cow — and must suffer the gregarious winners.

"For many years, people of this state hated Pitt, and most still do," said longtime West Virginia sportswriter Mickey Furfari, who has covered the Tech-WVU rivalry for four decades. "But today, the state is split. The southern half of the state looks forward to the Tech game. That's the one they want to win."

The schools are similar: Land-grant universities in mountain settings.

"They call the Pitt-WVU game the Backyard Brawl," said ESPN's Dr. Jerry Punch. "But this game is the Backwoods Brawl. They come out of the mountains to play this one."

---

uneasily quiet on the trip," senior end Lawrence Lewis said. "It kind of worried us because he's usually so talkative. But when he hit the field, he went crazy."

Even with a 6-2 record, Tech still had not found its way onto the national polls.

NOVEMBER 4:
TECH 31, NO. 20 SYRACUSE 7

ABC visited Blacksburg in a game hyped as the biggest in Lane Stadium history. It marked the first time ABC had done a game from Blacksburg since 1981. The Hokies were a bit wary; they were just 2-8 in games televised by that particular network.

The Orangemen entered the game with a 6-1 mark. Tech knew if it won, it would only have to beat Temple to ensure at least a share of the league championship.

The eighth-largest crowd (51,239) in Lane Stadium history snubbed the television sets and braved the cold to see Tech win in decisive fashion.

The Hokies allowed SU just 54 yards on the ground and

Middle linebacker George DelRicco punished West Virginia. In 1994, he landed a hit that jarred loose the ball, helmet and mouth-piece of quarterback Chad Johnston. In '95, he knocked the helmet off tight end Lovett Purnell.

After downing Big East rival Syracuse, Tech's fans downed a Lane Stadium goal post and paraded it through town.

167 total yards. The Orangemen had been averaging 381.3.

Earlier in the week ESPN college football analyst Craig "The Pony" James picked Syracuse to win because it had the "better quarterback" in freshman Donovan McNabb. So Tech's Druckenmiller threw for 224 yards, three touchdowns and no interceptions. He avoided sacks, looked off defenders and used the pump-fake to near-perfection. "I took [the comment] personally," Druckenmiller said.

Tech's "Death Row" defense keyed its Sugar Bowl Championship season.

The win put Tech (7-2 overall; 5-1 in the Big East) back in the Top 25: No. 19 in the USA Today/CNN Coaches poll and No. 21 in the Associated Press poll.

Cornell Brown was the Big East Defensive Player of the Week for an unprecedented second straight week (and third time this season) with nine tackles, three sacks and two forced fumbles. Tech held standout wideout Marvin Harrison to three catches for 51 yards and no scores by double-teaming him all game.

THE HELMET INCIDENT

Quarterback Jim Druckenmiller was besieged by fans following the Syracuse win. One asked to hold Druckenmiller's helmet while he signed some autographs, and the preoccupied quarterback sort of nodded. But when he had finished signing, the fan — and the helmet — were gone. So was Druckenmiller's mouthpiece, which was stuck in the faceguard.

"Lester [Karlin, Tech's equipment manager] would've issued me another helmet," Druckenmiller said. "But there's a psychological factor involved. A new one might have been uncomfortable. Plus I'm a little superstitious."

The story — complete with a plea from Druckenmiller to return the helmet — made the Saturday night TV newscasts and Sunday newspapers. Shamed, the fan/thief called Druckenmiller the next morning. "If I bring it over, you're not going to kick my butt, are you?" he asked. Druckenmiller assured him he would not.

Some time passed, and Druckenmiller heard some voices outside his apartment door. Then he heard a knock. "I think they were trying to decide whether they should just leave it at the doorstep or give it to me in person," Druckenmiller said.

The fan brought along some friends for moral support and apologized profusely. Then he asked Druckenmiller if he would mind signing his ticket stub and pose for some photographs.

"He was sorry about the whole thing," Druckenmiller said. "He said he had stood there with the helmet for awhile and when I didn't do anything, he figured I had given it to him.

"I was just glad to get it back. the mouthpiece, too. It saved me a trip to the dentist."

Jim Druckenmiller's helmet was safe this day as he signed post-game autographs. The same couldn't be said after Tech's 31-7 victory over the Orangemen.

DEATH ROW DEFENSE Fans and opponents alike were beginning to realize there was something special about this Tech defense, which dubbed itself "Death Row." You couldn't run right at the Hokies; the tackle rotation of Price, Jim Baron, Jeff Holland and Waverly Jackson was too big, strong and quick. And you couldn't ran around them; ends Brown, Hank Coleman and Lawrence Lewis were too quick and fast. Linebacker George DelRicco stuffed everything in the middle that got past the front line, and Newsome chased down everything on the sides. Heady Brandon Semones was always at the right place at the right time. The secondary of Larry Green, Antonio Banks, Torrian Gray and William Yarborough suffocated receivers and closed the gap on sweeps.

Going into Week 10, Tech had won its last four games by a combined score of 180-51. "We're kind of on a roll right now," co-defensive coordinator Bud Foster said. "Our kids have found a groove and stayed on it."

Ken Oxendine gained 593 yards and averaged 5.6 yards per carry in 1995.

NOVEMBER 11: TECH 38, TEMPLE 16

The Hokies, perhaps a little emotionally drained from their big victory the previous Saturday, started slowly at RFK Stadium and led just 10-6 after one quarter. But defensive tackles Jim Baron (46 yards) and J.C. Price (19 yards) scored touchdowns on consecutive possessions in the second quarter to break the game open. Baron picked up a fumble caused by Hank Coleman, while Price intercepted a screen pass and faked out Temple quarterback Pat Bonner with a nifty juke en route to the

end zone. "I was deciding whether I should blast him or not," Price said. "I had about five yards to go, and I thought if I tried to blast him I might fall down. I would've gotten joked on hard for that, so I decided to go around him. I guess that's where the move came from."

Tech clinched its first-ever Big East Championship with a 6-1 league mark (8-2 overall).

After the game Price and senior offensive tackle Mike Bianchin dumped a cooler of wet stuff over Beamer's head.

"I don't know if it was water or Gatorade," Beamer said, beaming. "But it was wet and it felt good."

Turns out it was water. "Lester would get mad at us if we wasted that much Gatorade," Price said.

Defensive tackle Jim Baron rumbles for a score against Temple in RFK Stadium.

NOVEMBER 18:
TECH 36, NO. 13 VIRGINIA 29

Going into the last week of the regular season, the stage was set for the most memorable — at least for the Hokies — game in the 100-year history of the Virginia Tech-Virginia series.

Cornell Brown put a hurtin' on Virginia's quarterbacks.

The No. 13 Cavaliers, 8-3, were co-champions of the ACC. The Hokies, 8-2, were co-champions of the Big East. Both schools shared the title with schools from the state of Florida, whom they had beaten. ABC picked up the game and would be televising it to 19.5 percent of the nation.

It might've been the greatest regular-season win in school history.

It came on the same field where Virginia had beaten No. 2 Florida State. The Cavaliers outgained the Hokies

Bryan Still was pumped for the 1995 Tech-UVa game.

420-319, collected nine more first downs, intercepted three passes and led for most of the way.

Things looked bad for the Hokies when, trailing 29-23, UVa's Todd White intercepted a Druckenmiller pass with 4:08 to play. "That should've been the difference," Virginia coach George Welsh said.

Tech needed to stop Virginia and get the ball back quickly. But on third-and-5 from the Tech 49-yard line, UVa quarterback Mike Groh threw downfield to tight end Bobby Neely. Tech strong safety Torrian Gray hit Neely before the ball arrived, giving the Cavaliers first-and-10 at the Tech 34-yard line with just 2:40 remaining. At that point, many members of the media packed up and left the press box for the field, thinking the game was over. "I thought that was our last chance," linebacker Brandon Semones said. "I thought Virginia would run out the clock."

UVa tried to do just that, but Tech fortunately still had all three of its time-outs.

Tailback Kevin Brooks rushed the right side for four yards, forcing Tech to use its first time-out at 2:30. Hank Coleman then dropped Brooks for a four-yard loss, and Tech took its second time-out at 2:24. "That was a big play," Tech co-defensive coordinator Bud Foster said. "It knocked Virginia out of easy field goal range."

Tailback Tiki Barber got five yards back on the next play, bringing up fourth-and-5. The Hokies burned their last time-out at 2:17.

Virginia lined up for a field-goal attempt, but holder Tim Sherman was set eight feet back instead of the normal seven. Welsh saw that his team was disorganized and called a time-out, a ploy ESPN later said "iced their own kicker."

Tech had beaten Virginia just twice in eight tries going into the '95 game (1990 and 1993).

Tech's 122 combined points against Akron and Rutgers set a school record for scoring in back-to-back games.

Blissful Tech fans carried Myron Newsome off the field at Scott Stadium.

Rafael Garcia's 47-yard attempt was wide left by about three feet. Down six with 2:12 to play, the Hokies were still alive — but with no time-outs.

Druckenmiller wasn't fazed. His first three passes fell incomplete, then on fourth-and-10 he looked off Virginia's middle linebacker and found Cornelius White across the middle for 14 yards. This was the same Cornelius White reviled by Tech fans for dropping big passes in the Hokies' first two games.

Druckenmiller got Tech to the Virginia 36-yard line, and offensive coordinator Rickey Bustle called the Pump and Go play. Split end Jermaine Holmes made a quick feint toward the outside. Druckenmiller pump-faked. Eager to make an interception, UVa free safety Percy Ellsworth bit on it. Holmes turned his route downfield. Druckenmiller heaved the ball and Holmes caught it between his wrists and coaxed it into his midsection before hitting the ground for a touchdown.

Atle Larsen converted the all-important extra point, and Tech led 30-29 with :47 left. Virginia threatened to score, but with :06 left, Tech's Antonio Banks stepped in front of a pass and raced 65 yards for a touchdown.

Tech now had won nine straight games. And, best of all, the Hokies had put themselves in position for a Bowl Alliance berth.

Frank Beamer's teams have a reputation for blocking kicks. Archie Hopkins blocked this one against Tulane in 1989.

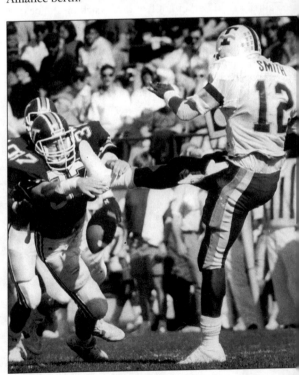

GREAT NO. 58

End Cornell Brown was Big East Defensive Player of the Week and *Sports Illustrated* National Defensive Player of the Week after he collected 12 tackles, two sacks and six quarterback pressures against Virginia — despite playing the game while he was recovering from the flu.

"I was groggy and my stomach was aching," he said. "I didn't eat much from Wednesday on and when I did I couldn't keep it down."

Brown's achievement marked the third time in four weeks he had captured the Big East award and the fifth straight week the honor had gone to a Hokie.

He finished the season with 103 tackles, including a league-high 25 for losses, and led the Big East with 14 sacks. He became Tech's fourth consensus All-American, joining Frank Loria (1967), Bruce Smith (1984) and Jim Pyne (1993).

His honors for 1995:
■ *Football News* National Defensive Player of the Year
■ Big East Conference Defensive Player of the Year
■ Associated Press First Team All-America
■ Football Writers Association First Team All-America
■ *Football News* First Team All-America
■ UPI First Team All-America
■ Dudley Award Winner as top collegiate player in Virginia
■ Tech team Most Valuable Player (for the second year in a row)
■ 1995-96 Hokie Huddler Athlete of the Year

Cornell Brown, right, was the shining star in a stellar Tech defensive unit.

GIECK OF THE WEEK As Banks raced down the left sideline — the Cavaliers' sideline — Virginia trainer Joe Gieck stuck out an orange polyester-panted leg in an effort to trip Banks. Was it a serious attempt to stop Banks? Or just a flippant gesture caused by the immediate frustration of realizing Tech had won? Either way, the unsportsmanlike action became big news. ESPN dubbed him the "Geek of the Week."

Virginia Tech's defense posted two shutouts on the road in 1995, the first time it had pulled off that feat since 1966.

HAVIN' A BLOCK PARTY The 1995 Tech squad blocked eight kicks, the most in Frank Beamer's nine seasons as head coach. The Hokies blocked at least one kick in five of their 11 games that season. The previous single-season best for blocks under Beamer was seven in 1988 when the Hokies blocked four punts and three field goals. Tech had six blocks in 1990, 1991, 1992 and 1993. The Hokies have 48 blocks in Beamer's 101 games as head coach: 21 punts, 15 field goals and 12 PATs.

Tech's 27-0 win over West Virginia marked the Mountaineers' worst home loss since 1976 and first home shutout since 1986.

POSTSEASON HONORS The Big East named Frank Beamer its Coach of the Year and Cornell Brown its Defensive Player of the Year in voting of the league's head coaches. Eleven Hokies made the All-Big East first or second teams, and five made first team: Brown, offensive guard Chris Malone, defensive tackle J.C. Price, linebacker George DelRicco and free safety William Yarborough. Second-teamers included quarterback Jim Druckenmiller, tailback Dwayne Thomas, center Billy Conaty, tackle Jay Hagood, linebacker Brandon Semones and strong safety Torrian Gray.

DOMINANT DEFENSE Tech's defense finished No. 1 nationally against the run, allowing just 77.4 yards per game. It ranked No. 5 in scoring defense (14.1 points) and No. 10 in total defense (285.9 yards per game). The Hokies led the Big East in rushing defense, scoring defense, total defense, third-down conversion defense and quarterback sacks.

In its last seven regular-season games, Tech registered 87 tackles behind the line of scrimmage, including 35 sacks.

Tech was one of just 11 football teams to win at least eight games in the '93, '94 and '95 seasons. The others were Florida State, Miami, Kansas State, Nebraska, Ohio State, Penn State, Alabama, Auburn, Florida and Texas A&M.

HIGH-OCTANE OFFENSE The Hokies' offense scored 321 points, the second-highest total in school history. Tech's scoring average of 29.2 points was its third-highest ever and its 4,233 yards of total offense ranked fourth all-time in school history.

WOULD HOKIES GET SNUBBED? Although the Hokies proved on the field they were the Big East's best team in 1995, their postseason destination was still in doubt.

Cornell Brown, scooping up this fumble, was the ringleader of Tech's awesome defense.

Because the Big East had no tiebreaker, both Tech and Miami tied for the league title — even though the Hokies won the head-to-head meeting. Tech had the better record (9-2 to 8-3) and was 3-0 against ranked teams (Miami was 0-3). Tech beat an ACC co-champ; Miami lost to an ACC co-champ. Tech was the higher-scoring team.

But the word was that if the Hurricanes — playing at home — beat Syracuse, the Orange Bowl would chose Miami over Tech. The Hokies were hoping for an SU win.

The Orangemen led 24-14 at halftime, but Miami roared back for a 35-24 victory.

"I thought we had no chance after that," Cornell Brown said. "I thought we were going back to the Gator Bowl."

Members of the media supported the Hokies. "If Virginia Tech isn't the Big East representative in the Alliance, it's a disgrace," ESPN's Mike Tirico said.

"If Virginia Tech isn't invited to an Alliance Bowl, it's a travesty and a farce," Beano Cook said on ESPN radio. "They beat Miami, didn't they? They just beat one of the best teams in the country on the road. How can you deny them?"

The first hint that Tech might not be dead came Sunday, when ESPN posted its predicted bowl matchups. The Hurricanes still weren't a lock for the

Roanoke Regional Airport was a busy place on Dec. 29, 1995, with 14 charters and more than 3,000 fans leaving for New Orleans. In all, 43 chartered flights left the state of Virginia for Louisiana.

Alliance, and Tech's name was still being bounced around. A glimmer of hope remained.

When he arrived at work Monday morning, Athletic Director Dave Braine thought for sure the Hokies were Gator-bound. By the end of the day he wasn't so sure.

Several factors were working. The Sugar Bowl committee made no secret that ticket sales were important to them. "The Sugar already has the TV money from the Alliance. They have to be concerned with selling tickets," veteran coordinating producer Ed Goren told *USA Today's* Rudy Martzke. "Let's say the Sugar Bowl does 1-2 ratings points lower with Virginia Tech than Florida State. It doesn't matter to the Sugar Bowl committee. The next year they get the national title game."

In Tuesday's USA Today, ESPN's Craig James predicted Tech vs. SWC champion in the Sugar Bowl. "To the Sugar Bowl people, Virginia Tech will fill the stadium and sell a lot of beer on Bourbon Street," he said.

"From the response I've gotten," he added, "the Hokies could sell out two stadiums."

Wednesday afternoon, all Braine would say was, "They're going to let us know something Friday. In the meantime, I'm going to get a good night's sleep."

He probably knew something then. Earlier that day the *Boston Globe* reported Miami would pull its football team from bowl consideration in hopes of avoiding future NCAA sanctions. The NCAA heard Miami's case two weeks earlier and had historically taken four to six weeks to reach a decision; a few weeks before, nobody expected the Hurricanes to receive its penalty in time to affect this season.

But — possibly spurred by Miami's commitment to stay home — the NCAA quickened its pace and meted out its sanctions that Friday. For violations under former coach Dennis Erickson, the Hurricanes lost 24 scholarships and were banned from postseason action for 1995.

The Hokies were in the Alliance.

SUGAR BOWL-BOUND Now the only question was where: Orange or Sugar? The Fiesta had the national championship game, so that was out.

Sugar Bowl representative Chuck Zatarain said his bowl talked with Orange representatives "24 hours a day" about possible matchups. "We had Florida State last year and we wanted two different teams."

As it turned out, the Orange took FSU, the Sugar took Texas, the Orange took Notre Dame, and the Sugar tabbed Tech. "Everything worked the way it should have," Zatarain said.

After an 0-2 start, the impossible had happened: Virginia Tech was going to the Sugar Bowl. In the most

Bryan Still was the Most Valuable Player of the 1995 Sugar Bowl.

improbable, exciting, crazy and impressive season in school history, Tech ran off nine straight wins and finished the regular season ranked No. 13 in the Associated Press poll. It had been unranked as late as Oct. 28.

Fans went nuts over the news. The Hokies sold 12,000 tickets the first two days and easily sold their allotment of 17,200 tickets. In all, an estimated 32,000 Tech fans made the trip to New Orleans.

DECEMBER 31: TECH 28, TEXAS 10

Would the Hokies be able to contain Texas' explosive "BMW Backfield" of quarterback James Brown and running backs Shon Mitchell and Ricky Williams? Could they move the ball against a sturdy defensive front led by All-America Tony Brackens and 6-1, 292-pound noseguard Chris Akins? Those were the questions Tech fans were asking heading into the big game.

The Hokies looked a little stale for most of the first half and trailed, 10-0. Then Bryan Still made what

On Jan. 2, Tech learned it had won the Lambert Trophy as the top team in the East for 1995. Tech received 69 votes, edging Penn State, which received 64.

Larry Green carried a Tech victory flag around the Superdome.

The Hokies won five games on the road for the first time since 1966.

In the two showdowns prior to the 1995 Tech-UVa game, the team that lost went to a higher-paying bowl than the winner.

ultimately was the Play of the Game when he returned a punt 60 yards for a score with 2:34 left in the half. "We were playing fairly awful in the first half," Beamer said, "Then all of a sudden we get the punt return touchdown and we're down three."

Still — the game's MVP — set up Tech's go-ahead touchdown with a 27-yard catch to the Texas 2-yard line late in the third quarter. Then he helped break the game open with a 54-yard scoring catch with 12:28 left to put Tech up, 21-10. Tech's defense did the rest, sacking Brown five times and intercepting him three times.

Texas offensive tackle John Elmore said things fell apart when Tech applied its second-half defensive pressure. "We couldn't stop it," he said. "It's like when you have three holes that are leaking but only two fingers to try and stop it."

Hokie junior tackle Jay Hagood earned the respect of Texas All-America end Tony Brackens. "Hagood is the best pass blocker I've faced," he said. "His run-blocking is about the same as anyone else but his pass-blocking is definitely the best."

The Hokies' Holy Trinity of Football Success: The Sugar Bowl, Lambert and Big East Championship trophies.

BIG EAST; BIG PAYOFF "I said in 1991 that the Big East would be good for Virginia Tech, but that Tech would be good for the Big East, too," Beamer said after the Hokies defeated Texas, 28-10, at Louisiana's Superdome.

"We are here tonight because of the Big East. It's given us great opportunities. But the Big East is a better football conference tonight because of this football team, because we had over 30,000 fans here, and because we played and defeated a great Texas football team."

Not only had Tech become a member of a great conference, but it had become the league's brightest new star.

The Hokies' nine straight wins in 1995 set a school record.

Voices

TECH ON THE AIR

18. Name Tech's five first-team All-Big East selections in 1995.

Through the years, Virginia Tech fans have followed the Hokies on radio through the descriptions of a series of talented broadcasters, many of whom have gone on to gain national fame.

The Tech network dates back to 1954, when Radford radio station WRAD began broadcasting Tech sports. Joe Knakel and Bob Bradford called the first-ever Tech football radio broadcast, a 30-21 victory over North Carolina State. In the booth that day were producer Tom Gannaway and spotter Ralph Price.

Price didn't stray far from the Tech radio booth for the next 40 years, serving as the network's spotter and statistician.

"In 1955 we played at Pennsylvania, and their stadium held about 100,000 people," Price said. "Our radio booth was at the 20-yard line and when the ball was on the other end of the field, you couldn't even see the jersey numbers of the players. You couldn't tell who had the ball. We had some guessing to do that day."

THE WRNL-ERA In 1957, Richmond station WRNL, led by station manager Frank Soden, took over the network and expanded to 43 stations.

Soden hired Frank Messer as the new voice of the Hokies. "He had a great voice and really knew the game well," Soden said.

Eventually, Messer left Virginia for New York as the voice of the New York Yankees and called World Series games in 1977 and 1978. He also called games for CBS Radio.

Frank Soden served as the Tech Network coordinator and analyst for 13 seasons.

Messer was replaced in 1961 by Bob Gillmore, who had worked Cincinnati Reds radio broadcasts with Waite Hoyt before ending up in Richmond.

From 1963-1971, Charlie Harville and Soden made up the Tech radio crew. The two worked Tech's first-ever bowl game, the 1966 Liberty Bowl game with Miami.

Soden's work on the Tech network was truly remarkable. His 13-year run as analyst is the second longest tenure of any Tech broadcaster. He became an institution in Richmond for his work with the University of Richmond and with the Richmond Braves baseball club.

Because Soden was one of the most respected broadcasters in state history, the Frank Soden Lifetime

Achievement Award is awarded each year to the person who has contributed the most to broadcasting in Richmond.

'THIS ONE BELONGS TO THE REDS!' In the early 1960s Tech basketball games were also broadcast by young Dave Van Horn. He and Tech sports information director/analyst Wendy Weisend were there when Bill Matthews — in his first game as coach — defeated Kentucky in Lexington, 80-77.

Van Horn called Tech basketball for five seasons and filled in on some football broadcasts with Soden during the 1968 season.

But baseball was Van Horn's calling, and when Major League Baseball expanded in 1969 to Montreal, he became the English voice of the Expos. He's still calling the Expos games today.

By the mid-1970s, Tech football was getting bigger and bigger. So in 1973 Frank Moseley hired the state's premier broadcaster as its new voice: Marty Brennaman, a 31-year old Portsmouth native and radio and TV voice of the Virginia Squires of the ABA.

Brennaman — a three-time Virginia Sportscaster of the Year — was teamed with Don Lloyd Fleeger, station manager of Blacksburg's WKEX-AM.

Brennaman left after one season to become voice of the Cincinnati Reds. Two years later, the Big Red

HOKIES QUIZ

19. What color combination will Virginia Tech never wear again as long as Frank Beamer is head coach?

Marty Brennaman (right) and Don Fleeger composed Tech's broadcast team in 1973.

Ken Haines was a key broadcast figure for the Hokies in the 1970s.

Machine captured the World Series in a dramatic series win over Boston.

"This one belongs to the Reds" became Brennaman's trademark call after each Red's victory, a phrase he still uses today in his role as the Reds radio announcer.

Don Lloyd Fleeger — air name Don Lloyd — was the first broadcaster to call both Tech football and basketball on a consistent basis. Hailing from Ohio, Fleeger had 20 years experience, including three as the play-by-play announcer for William & Mary. As the station manager of the Blacksburg station, he was the voice of Tech sports from 1974-1982.

In 1975, Tech's network grew considerably under the direction of Ken Haines, the university's Director of Public Affairs.

Haines served as the color analyst on Tech football and some basketball games with Fleeger. The size of the network tripled with nearly 50 stations carrying every Tech football game each Saturday.

'THAT WAS A 'SWEEP-STYLE' PLAY, JEFF'

In 1983 Jeff Charles replaced Fleeger as Tech's radio voice. Like Fleeger, Charles was from Ohio. He came to Tech from Furman University where he had been that school's voice after working at Atlanta radio station WSB.

Along with handling the radio broadcasts, Charles hosted the "Bill Dooley Show," a weekly television program featuring Tech's head football coach.

The show was often taped in the wee hours of the morning. Every Tech fan could imitate Dooley's North Carolina drawl and mannerisms that aired on every Sunday show. To wit: Dooley loved to add the word

Jeff Charles, right, was the Voice of the Hokies from 1983-87. He is shown with Coach Bill Dooley.

"style" to describe the action, as in "sweep-style" play or "draw-style" play.

Today, Charles is the voice of the East Carolina University Pirates.

THE SINGING BANDIT One of Charles' first moves at Tech was bringing in former Tech tight end Mike Burnop to serve as football color analyst.

In 1995 in a game at Navy, Burnop added a twist to his presentation. As the Navy band played "Anchor's Aweigh," Burnop started humming, then singing along with the band. After Tech won the game, fans on the network's postgame talk show, "The Point-After," applauded Mike's selection.

The work of analyst Mike Burnop — a former star Hokie tight end — is music to Tech fans' ears.

The following week, Tech played the Akron Zips. Burnop sang "Zippity-Do-Dah." Tech won again.

By now, Tech fans and the media picked up on the act. The *Richmond Times-Dispatch* ran a feature — not on his exceptional analysis of the games — but his choice of melodies each week.

As long as Tech won, Burnop would sing. And as long as he sang, Tech kept winning.

The Hokies put together a 10-game winning streak. Burnop had to keep churning out the tunes.

Tech 27, West Virginia 0: "Almost Heaven, West Virginia."

Tech 31, Syracuse 7: "New York, New York."

The wins and the songs kept coming. Although the melodies were familiar, Burnop would change the lyrics depending on the opponent.

Before the Hokies played in the Sugar Bowl, Tech coach Frank Beamer promised he'd sing along with Burnop if the Hokies beat Texas. Sure enough, Tech won, meaning Beamer and Burnop had to perform a duet following the Hokies' 28-10 win.

HOKIES QUIZ

20. Name Virginia Tech's four consensus All-Americans.

The melody was 'The Yellow Rose of Texas."
The lyrics were:

Oh the Hokies went to New Orleans
to play a football game
The Sugar Bowl had chosen
the teams to entertain.
The Texas Guys were awesome,
Self-assured and unafraid.
The Hokies were just happy
to be in the parade.
But, the Yellow Rose of Texas
has turned Maroon tonight.
The Hokies beat the Longhorns,
this game was outta sight!

So Frank Beamer became the first coach in history to

win the Sugar Bowl and then have to sing about it on his postgame radio show.

'TOUCHDOWN, TECH' In 1988 Bill Roth replaced Charles as "Voice of the Hokies." Roth, 22, had been the radio voice at Marshall University the previous season.

By the end of 1996, Roth will have broadcast more Tech football and basketball games than any other announcer in school history.

Roth is known for two signature lines: his opening to every Tech broadcast, "From the Blue Waters of the

THE BEAM TEAM

The best players under coach Frank Beamer, chosen by *The Hokie Huddler*.

OFFENSE

QB Jim Druckenmiller — Led Tech to greatest season ever.

TB Dwayne Thomas — Ranks fourth all-time on Tech's career rushing list. Great intangibles. A winner: three years as a starter, three bowls.

FB Brian Edmonds — Like Thomas, a winner. Excellent rusher and blocker.

TE John Burke — He is to tight ends what Tony Paige was to Tech fullbacks. A devastating blocker, great leader and still playing in the NFL.

SE Antonio Freeman — Tech's career pass receiving leader and now a member of the Green Bay Packers.

FL/KR Bryan Still — Mr. Big Play. MVP of the Sugar Bowl. San Diego's top pick in 1996.

OL Jim Pyne — Tech's only unanimous All-American.

OL Todd Grantham — Went on to become a great coach as well.

OL Eugene Chung — A first-round NFL draft choice.

OL Billy Conaty — The next Pyne?

OL William Boatwright — He was strong as a battleship.

PK Ryan Williams — Tech's all-time scoring leader.

DEFENSE

DE Cornell Brown — Greatest player ever under Beamer.

DE Jimmy Whitten — Only defender ever to start 44 straight games.

DT J.C. Price — Blood and guts of Sugar Bowl Champion squad.

DT Scott Hill — He was J.C. Price before J.C. Price.

LB Ken Brown — A do-it-all player who led Tech in tackles in 1994.

LB George DelRicco — A close call over Randy Cockrell.

LB Myron Newsome — One of Beamer's most talented players ever.

CB Tyronne Drakeford — Still playing with San Francisco.

CB Antonio Banks — Has scored some of the biggest touchdowns in school history. And a vicious hitter.

SS Torrian Gray — Three years, three bowls, great leader.

FS William Yarborough — "Killer" was a thriller.

P Robbie Colley — His average improved every year (38.1 — 38.4 — 42.1).

Chesapeake Bay to the Hills of Tennessee, the Virginia Tech Hokies are on the air!"

And every Hokie fan loves to hear him say "Touchdown, Tech!" — and the more, the better.

Roth — who won the distinguished Robert Costas Scholarship as an undergraduate at Syracuse in 1986 — was named 1995 Virginia Sportscaster of the Year.

THE MEDIA

The unsung heroes of any football program are the sports information directors. They work tirelessly during the season, every weekend, with no day off. They are the center of the media hurricane covering a collegiate team: lining up interviews, serving press, radio and television members, making contacts, pounding out fact sheets, answering questions and running up huge phone and fax bills.

For most of the modern era of Tech football, the Hokies have had just two men in charge: Wendy Weisend, who reigned from 1956-78, and Jack Williams, who has been Tech's SID since 1978.

A legend among members of the press, Wendell Holmes Weisend was a graduate of Ohio Wesleyan University who earned his master's degree in journalism from Northwestern in 1951.

In July 1983, he was elected to the College Sports Information Directors Hall of Fame. He later became the first person from the public relations field chosen for the Tech Hall of Fame when he was inducted in 1991.

During his tenure, Weisend saw huge growth in Virginia Tech's football program: the move from Miles to Lane Stadium, the advent of television exposure and the blossoming of Tech's first long-standing intersectional rivalry.

"The Florida State series was important to the development of Virginia Tech football," Weisend said. "There was no home schedule to speak of before that. Those FSU games were crucial. The Hokies got beat a lot, but they also won a lot of those games. Even just playing well against FSU gave them confidence, and gave them recognition among folks who knew what was going on."

Weisend said he believes he knows why Tech was never asked to join the Atlantic Coast Conference.

"In 1949, Tech President Walter Newman was also president of the Southern Conference," he said. "It was a hoity-toity league that didn't believe in postseason action, and when Clemson wanted to play in a bowl game, the league said no. Newman signed the paperwork blocking the bid, incensing Clemson Athletic Director Frank Howard.

Bill Roth was 22 years old when he joined Tech in 1988. He has broadcast more Tech football and basketball games than any other announcer in school history.

Wendy Weisend: a Hall of Fame sports information director.

"In 1953, North Carolina, Duke, Wake Forest, North Carolina State, South Carolina and Maryland broke away from the Southern Conference to form the ACC. Just as Newman blocked Clemson's bowl bid, Howard — who was otherwise a good man — blocked Tech's invitation into the ACC."

Weisend was a success outside the world of sports as well. He received the Purple Heart and Distinguished Flying Cross for service in World War II, during which he flew 28 missions as a gunner with the Eighth Air Force and earned the Air Medal with three clusters.

WILLIAMS: A STALWART SINCE '78 Tech Director of Media

CHRIS COLSTON'S TOP 20 GREATEST TECH

How do you judge one game against another? I used three criteria: quality of opponent, impact on the season and excitement of the game.

Notice that most of the games on my list are from the 1970s-on. That's when I started following Tech football (I like to stick with what I know). Also, some games might have more personal significance for me than they might for someone else. Surely this isn't a definitive list. If it causes a few arguments at the local tavern, then it has served its purpose:

1. TEXAS (28-10, 1995): This Sugar Bowl victory over the No. 9 ranked Longhorns is Virginia Tech's greatest athletics achievement.

2. NORTH CAROLINA STATE (25-24, 1986): If a game can make Dave Smith cry, it has to be high on the list.

3. VIRGINIA (36-29, 1995): This one had it all: nationally-ranked opponent (UVa was No. 13), state rivalry, excitement and impact. With the win the Hokies jumped from No. 20 to No. 13 in the AP rankings.

4. MIAMI (13-7, 1995): The Hokies were 0-2 and slumping with the No. 17 Hurricanes coming to town. This game turned everything around. Perhaps it changed the course of Virginia Tech football; time will tell.

5. INDIANA (45-20, 1993): Bowl wins justify a season and legitimize a program. This Independence victory over the No. 21 Hoosiers was one of Tech's wildest wins ever.

6. CLEMSON (20-14, 1986): The Hokies were 12 ½-point underdogs and had not won in Death Valley since 1954. The Tigers finished the season ranked No. 17 in the AP. This game set the tone for the Peach Bowl Championship season.

7. FLORIDA STATE (20-11, 1964): This was Bob Schweickert's great punting game and the one where frustrated Seminole Fred Biletnikoff winged the ball into the top row of tiny Miles Stadium. FSU was ranked No. 10 in the nation.

8. VIRGINIA (48-0, 1983): There were more significant wins over Virginia, but none felt this good. A total domination of the state rival on a gloriously sunny day — in Charlottesville, no less.

Relations Jack Williams arrived with Bill Dooley in 1978 from the University of North Carolina.

In nine years as SID at UNC, Williams helped the Tar Heels get three consensus All-Americans and two others who made first team All-America on at least one squad. At Tech his work was influential in bringing the Outland Trophy to Bruce Smith.

Williams has a rich bank of Hokie football memories.

The news of Dooley's first bowl bid at Tech was memorable for Williams in more ways than one. "It was 1980, and we had beaten VMI in Norfolk's Oyster Bowl," he said. "Former Georgia Tech running back Johnny Gresham was on the Peach Bowl committee. After the

FOOTBALL VICTORIES

9. WEST VIRGINIA (12-10, 1989): It was the Hokies' first road win over a Top 10 opponent in the modern era. WVU was ranked No. 9.

10. KENTUCKY (17-15, 1986): Tech drove from its own 5-yard line to the Wildcat 32-yard line, then with no time left Chris Kinzer kicked a 49-yard field goal in the mud. Was the Peach in the balance?

11. VIRGINIA (38-13, 1990): An ESPN night audience saw Tech whip the No. 17 Cavaliers, who earlier in the season had been ranked No. 1 in the country.

12. VIRGINIA (30-0, 1980): This was the game that turned Bill Dooley's program around and was Tech's first blowout win (i.e., more than 17 points) over UVa since 1961.

13. DUKE (22-21, 1982): Down 21-0, Tech stormed back, then scored with 33 seconds left to make it 21-20. The Hokies went for the two-point conversion — and made it.

14. SYRACUSE (31-7, 1995): Billed as one of the biggest games in Lane Stadium history, Tech pretty much sealed its first Big East title with this win over the No. 20 Orangemen.

15. OKLAHOMA STATE (34-32, 1972): Tech trailed 32-31 with less than a minute to play. With 12 seconds left Dave Strock attempted a field goal but missed to the right. Officials called the No. 19 Cowboys offside, and he converted the 18-yarder for a 34-32 win.

16. FLORIDA STATE (23-21, 1966): A win almost as good as the one in '64.

17. GEORGETOWN (3-0, 1941): The No. 2 Hoyas were defending national champions, but Tech pulled off a shocking surprise.

18. GEORGIA (7-6, 1932): A big win over a true Southern power. The Associated Press didn't begin ranking teams until 1936, but Georgia would've been high up there.

19. KENTUCKY (7-0, 1932): Ditto. Kentucky had quite a team that year.

20. VIRGINIA (11-0, 1905): This was the game in which Hunter Carpenter finally beat the Cavaliers. The loss so irked UVa that it wouldn't play Tech for 17 years.

game we went down in this little cramped locker room. Bill Dooley introduced him and the players went wild. Back then a bowl bid was big-time special. Tech hadn't been to a bowl since 1968 and it was something to behold. Remember, those guys were awful in 1978 and 1979 and had no idea they were ever going to a bowl.

"The players picked up Johnny Gresham and started carrying him around the room. He tried to talk but was drowned out by the players chanting 'Peach Bowl! Peach Bowl! Peach Bowl!' There were these big 270-pound guys carrying him around the room and they whacked me against the wall. The celebration resulted in a broken rib for me but it was worth it. In 50 years of athletics, I've never been involved in anything more exciting than that moment."

Another Peach Bowl memory stands tall for Williams. "The thing I remember about the 1986 Peach Bowl was [placekicker] Chris Kinzer holding an audience in the hotel lobby after the [25-24] win," he said. "He must've talked to 10,000 people wanting autographs. It was like he didn't want that moment to ever end.

"That game was Dooley's coup de grâce. He had been canned by the university then won his last game in exciting fashion. That was more dramatic than anything he did at North Carolina. It was the kind of story if you made a movie about it, people would say it was 'corny.' It was a Grade B movie script, except it actually happened."

Williams believed there could've been more big moments at Tech under Dooley, but his schedules nixed that. "I wish Dooley had played more big-time oppon-ents," Williams said. "We played too many smaller state schools and never got the credit we could've received."

All that changed with membership in the Big East, the biggest development Williams has seen during his time at Tech. "Joining the Big East was like someone waving a magic wand over our heads," he said. "If we were an independent, we'd probably still be struggling.

"When I first came here in 1978, if anyone had suggested that Virginia Tech would go to the Sugar Bowl and beat Texas, I would've laughed at them and told them they were crazy. In 1978 that was an unreachable goal. The Big East made it reachable."

MR. SMITH GOES TO BLACKSBURG Sports information director Dave Smith arrived in Blacksburg in the summer of 1975 and has worked under both Weisend and Williams. He's seen more than 200 Tech football games, 350 basketball contests and 1,100 baseball games, and he is regarded by the media as a walking encyclopedia of Hokie knowledge.

Although he said the Sugar Bowl was the "most fun"

Dave Smith, left, and Jack Williams, right: a dynamic duo for 18 years — and counting.

he's had with Tech and was the school's "defining moment," his most emotional Hokie experience came in the 1986 Peach Bowl. "That was special," he said. "I was in the TV booth spotting for the broadcasting crew. When N.C. State called the time-out to try and ice Chris Kinzer, the analyst, Lee Corso, turned to me and asked, 'Can he make it?' I told him, 'Yes. He's done it all year.'

"After Kinzer made the kick, I was overwhelmed emotionally. I was so happy I was crying. Other than the NIT Championship, there hadn't been anything of that magnitude happen to Virginia Tech."

Joining the Hokies' athletics department was a dream come true for Smith, a Tech graduate. He met Weisend through the course of his job and became a candidate when an opening arose in the summer of 1975.

Smith — then a sportswriter with the *Franklin County News-Post* — was riding to an event with *Roanoke Times* sportswriter Mark Meng.

"I'm thinking about getting into sports information," Smith said.

"You don't want to do that,' Meng said, shaking his head. "Those guys don't get paid anything, they work long hours and they all have heart problems and die young."

Smith took the job anyway — at a pay cut. And he was making less than $10,000 a year at the newspaper.

He hasn't had heart trouble and he now makes more than $10,000 a year. But he still works those long hours.

HOKIES QUIZ

23. When did Tech have its only undefeated football season?

By the Numbers

The statistics found here are provided by the Virginia Tech Sports Information department and are updated through the 1995-96 school year.

SEASON-BY-SEASON SUMMARY

Year	Coach	W	L	T	Captain(s)
1892	E.A. Smyth	1	1	0	W.E. Anderson
1893	E.A. Smyth	0	2	0	S.V. Lovenstein
1894	J.A. Massie	4	1	0	T.D. Martin
1895	A.C. Jones	4	2	0	J.L. Ingles
1896	A.C. Jones	5	2	1	J.L. Ingles
1897	C. Firth	5	2	0	H.A. Johnson
1898	J.L. Ingles	3	2	0	C.M. Wood
1899	Dr. James Morrison	4	1	0	W.F. Cox
1900	Dr. Davis	3	3	1	J.B. Huffard
1901	Dr. A.B. Morrison, Jr.	6	1	0	C.J.B. DeCamps
1902	R.R. Brown	3	2	1	C.H. Carpenter
1903	Dr. C.A. Lueder	5	1	0	C.P. Miles
1904	J.C. O'Connor	5	3	0	G.C. Wilson
1905	C.P. Miles	9	1	0	T.W. Lewis
1906	C.P. Miles	5	2	2	J.A. Nutter
1907	C.R. Williams	7	2	0	C.E. Diffendal
1908	R.M. Brown	5	4	0	Joe Luttrell
1909	B.B. Bocock	6	1	0	E.R. Hodgson
1910	B.B. Bocock	6	2	0	V.B. Hodgson
1911	L.W. Reiss	6	1	2	A.G. Gibbs
1912	B.B. Bocock	5	4	0	W.H. Burruss
1913	B.B. Bocock	7	1	1	L.A. Pick
1914	B.B. Bocock	6	2	1	M.F. Peak, Jr.
1915	B.B. Bocock	4	4	0	V.F. Dixon
1916	J.E. Ingersell	7	2	0	J.S. Caffee
1917	C.A. Bernier	6	2	1	H.T. Parrish
1918	C.A. Bernier	7	0	0	H. Crisp, D. Roden
1919	C.A. Bernier	5	4	0	J.T. Hardwick
1920	S.B. Sutton	4	6	0	H.B. Redd
1921	B.C. Cubbage	7	3	0	S.D. Tilson
1922	B.C. Cubbage	8	1	1	H.J. Hardwick
1923	B.C. Cubbage	6	3	0	H.M. Sutton
1924	B.C. Cubbage	4	2	3	S.O. Graham
1925	B.C. Cubbage	5	3	2	J.H. Moran
1926	A.F. Gustafson	5	3	1	J.H. Moran
1927	A.F. Gustafson	5	4	0	V.E. Miles
1928	A.F. Gustafson	7	2	0	A.E. Bailey
1929	A.F. Gustafson	5	4	0	L.B. Nutter
1930	O.E. Neale	5	3	1	H.V. Hooper
1931	O.E. Neale	3	4	2	C.E. Brown
1932	H.B. Redd	8	1	0	W. Grinus, Jr.
1933	H.B. Redd	4	3	3	Bill Porterfield
1934	H.B. Redd	5	5	0	George Smith
1935	H.B. Redd	4	3	2	Louis Fittro
1936	H.B. Redd	5	5	0	Dave Jones
1937	H.B. Redd	5	5	0	C.L. Shockey
1938	H.B. Redd	3	5	2	Frank Pierce
1939	H.B. Redd	4	5	1	Dave Pitts, Jim Coleman
1940	H.B. Redd	5	5	0	John Henderson, William Zydiak
1941	J.R. Kitts	6	4	0	William M. Tate
1942	H.M. McEver	7	2	1	W. James, S.D. Tilson
1945	H.M. McEver	2	6	0	Floyd Bowles
1946	J.R. Kitts	3	4	3	Elmer Wilson
1947	J.R. Kitts	4	5	0	Bill Barbour, Bobby Smith
1948	R.C. McNeish	0	8	1	Tom Burns, Oren Hopkins
1949	R.C. McNeish	1	7	2	Jack Ittner, Bruce Fisher
1950	R.C. McNeish	0	10	0	Ron Casto
1951	F.O. Moseley	2	8	0	(none)
1952	F.O. Moseley	5	6	0	(none)

Year	Coach	W	L	T	Captain(s)
1953	F.O. Moseley	5	5	0	(none)
1954	F.O. Moseley	8	0	1	Billy Kerfoot, Howie Wright
1955	F.O. Moseley	6	3	1	Dickie Beard, Jack Prater
1956	F.O. Moseley	7	2	1	Don Divers
1957	F.O. Moseley	4	6	0	Corbin Bailey
1958	F.O. Moseley	5	4	1	Jim Burks
1959	F.O. Moseley	6	4	0	Carroll Dale
1960	F.O. Moseley	6	4	0	Allen Whittier
1961	J.D. Claiborne	4	5	0	Terry Strock, Joe Moss
1962	J.D. Claiborne	5	5	0	Dave Gillespie, Aster Sizemore
1963	J.D. Claiborne	8	2	0	Gene Breen, Newt Green
1964	J.D. Claiborne	6	4	0	Vic Kreiter, Darrell Page, Bob Schweickert
1965	J.D. Claiborne	7	3	0	Billy Edwards, Bobby Owens, Mike Saunders
1966	J.D. Claiborne	8	2	1	Dave Farmer, Tommy Groom, Sands Woody
1967	J.D. Claiborne	7	3	0	Bob Griffith, Frank Loria
1968	J.D. Claiborne	7	4	0	Frank Beamer, Ron Davidson, Waddey Harvey
1969	J.D. Claiborne	4	5	1	Jerry Green, Pete Dawyot, Steve Bocko
1970	J.D. Claiborne	5	6	0	Jim Pigninelli, Perry Tiberio
1971	C.E. Coffey	4	7	0	Game Captains
1972	C.E. Coffey	6	4	1	Game Captains
1973	C.E. Coffey	2	9	0	Game Captains
1974	Jimmy Sharpe	4	7	0	Randy Vey, Charlie Martin
1975	Jimmy Sharpe	8	3	0	Doug Thacker, Phil Rogers
1976	Jimmy Sharpe	6	5	0	Paul Adams, Mitcheal Barnes, Tom Beasley
1977	Jimmy Sharpe	3	7	1	Rick Razzano, Roscoe Coles, Bill Houseright, George Roberts
1978	Bill Dooley	4	7	0	Dennis Scott, Chip Keatley
1979	Bill Dooley	5	6	0	Kenny Lewis, Mickey Fitzgerald, Mike Faulkner, Danny Hill
1980	Bill Dooley	8	4	0	Sidney Snell, Paul Davis, Lewis Stuart
1981	Bill Dooley	7	4	0	Steve Casey, Robert Brown
1982	Bill Dooley	7	4	0	Padro Phillips, Rick Miley, Mark Udinski
1983	Bill Dooley	9	2	0	Mike Johnson, Tony Paige
1984	Bill Dooley	8	4	0	Ashley Lee, Bruce Smith, Joe Jones
1985	Bill Dooley	6	5	0	Kent Thomas, Rainer Coleman
1986	Bill Dooley	10	1	1*	Maurice Williams, Curtis Taliaferro
1987	Frank Beamer	2	9	0	Erik Chapman, Steve Johnson, Kevin Keeffe, Carter Wiley
1988	Frank Beamer	3	8	0	Todd Grantham, Randy Cockrell, Scott Hill, Horacio Moronta, Bobby Martin
1989	Frank Beamer	6	4	1	Scott Hill, Randy Cockrell, Bobby Martin, Brian McCall
1990	Frank Beamer	6	5	0	Nick Cullen, Jimmy Whitten, Archie Hopkins, Al Chamblee
1991	Frank Beamer	5	6	0	Phil Bryant, Eugene Chung, William Boatwright, Wooster Pack
1992	Frank Beamer	2	8	1	Mark Poindexter, Rusty Pendleton, Melendez Byrd, Jerome Preston
1993	Frank Beamer	9	3	0	Jim Pyne, Tyronne Drakeford, John Burke, Joe Swarm, Bernard Basham
1994	Frank Beamer	8	4	0	Ken Brown, Maurice DeShazo, Antonio Freeman, Damien McMahon, Ranall White
1995	Frank Beamer	10	2	0	J.C. Price, George DelRicco, Hank Coleman, Mike Bianchin, Jermaine Holmes

* Includes a forfeit by Temple.

COACHING RECORDS

Name	Seasons	W	L	T	Pct.	Years
Bill Dooley	9	64	37	1	.632	1978-86
Jerry Claiborne	10	61	39	2	.608	1961-70
Frank Moseley	10	54	42	4	.560	1951-60
Frank Beamer	9	51	49	2	.510	1987-
H.B. Redd	9	43	37	8	.534	1932-40
Branch Bocock	6	34	14	2	.680	1909-10; 1912-15
Ben Cubbage	5	30	12	6	.688	1921-25
Andy Gustafson	4	22	13	1	.625	1926-29
Jimmy Sharpe	4	21	22	1	.489	1974-77
Charles Bernier	3	18	6	1	.740	1917-19
C.P. Miles	2	14	3	2	.737	1905-06
James Kitts	3	13	13	3	.500	1941; 1946-47
Charlie Coffey	3	12	20	1	.379	1971-73
A.C. Jones	2	9	4	1	.679	1895-96
H.M. McEver	2	9	8	1	.528	1942; 1945

Name	Seasons	W	L	T	Pct.	Years
O.E. Neale	2	8	7	3	.528	1930-31
C.R. Williams	1	7	2	0	.778	1907
Jack Ingersell	1	7	2	0	.778	1916
A.B. Morrison, Jr.	1	6	1	0	.857	1901
L.W. Reiss	1	6	1	2	.778	1911
C.A. Lueder	1	5	1	0	.833	1903
Charles Firth	1	5	2	0	.714	1897
John C. O'Conner	1	5	3	0	.625	1904
R.M. Brown	1	5	4	0	.556	1908
J.A. Massie	1	4	1	0	.800	1894
James Morrison	1	4	1	0	.800	1899
Stanley Sutton	1	4	6	0	.400	1920
J.L. Ingles	1	3	2	0	.600	1898
R.R. Brown	1	3	2	1	.583	1902
Dr. Davis	1	3	3	1	.500	1900
E.A. Smyth	2	1	3	0	.250	1892-93
Robert McNeish	3	1	25	3	.086	1948-50

YEARLY LEADERS

RUSHING

Year	Player	Carries	Yds.	TDs
1952	Don Welsh	102	392	2
1953	Dickie Beard	60	349	1
1954	Dickie Beard	128	647	2
1955	Dickie Beard	92	382	2
1956	Bobby Wolfenden	74	459	4
1957	Corbin Bailey	89	366	0
1958	Pat Henry	78	375	5
1959	Alger Pugh	112	615	6
1960	Warren Price	98	350	5
1961	Warren Price	93	356	3
1962	Gerald Bobbitte	95	312	3
1963	Bob Schweickert	155	839	7
1964	Sonny Utz	175	777	10
1965	Bobby Owens	146	526	7
1966	Tommy Francisco	203	753	13
1967	Terry Smoot	68	356	4
1968	Terry Smoot	196	820	8
1969	Terry Smoot	246	940	11
1970	Perry Tiberio	184	764	8
1971	James Barber	93	501	9
1972	James Barber	186	624	13
1973	Phil Rogers	175	1036	1
1974	Phil Rogers	153	663	7
1975	Roscoe Coles	194	1045	10
1976	Roscoe Coles	209	1119	9
1977	Roscoe Coles	158	672	4
1978	Kenny Lewis	184	1020	10
1979	Cyrus Lawrence	177	791	9
1980	Cyrus Lawrence	271	1221	8
1981	Cyrus Lawrence	325	1403	8
1982	Billy Hite	145	622	3
1983	Otis Copeland	158	709	7
1984	Maurice Williams	149	574	6
1985	Maurice Williams	167	936	9
1986	Maurice Williams	166	1029	6
1987	Jon Jeffries	125	599	3
1988	Ralph Brown	140	514	4
1989	Vaughn Hebron	134	584	1
1990	Vaughn Hebron	133	640	3
1991	Tony Kennedy	143	684	10
1992	Vaughn Hebron	105	579	5
1993	Dwayne Thomas	214	1130	11
1994	Dwayne Thomas	142	655	5
1995	Dwayne Thomas	167	673	7

PASSING

Year	Player	Comp-Att	Yds.	TDs	Int.
1952	Johnny Dean	62-136	878	2	17
1953	Johnny Dean	26-62	314	0	6
1954	Billy Cranwell	18-37	316	7	6
1955	Billy Cranwell	25-54	458	4	5
1956	Jimmy Lugar	32-76	556	6	8
1957	Billy Cranwell	36-57	391	0	2
1958	Billy Holsclaw	70-127	1013	9	7
1959	Frank Eastman	32-68	548	10	8
1960	Warren Price	29-73	386	7	7
1961	Warren Price	37-93	381	5	5
1962	Pete Cartwright	26-60	266	3	3
1963	Bob Schweickert	62-116	687	6	8
1964	Bob Schweickert	52-109	833	9	3
1965	Bobby Owens	68-122	891	6	7
1966	Tommy Stafford	53-113	610	5	6
1967	Al Kincaid	64-132	556	3	6
1968	Al Kincaid	47-97	537	2	5
1969	Bob German	51-105	743	2	8
1970	Gil Schwabe	61-126	815	5	7
1971	Don Strock	195-356	2577	12	19
1972	Don Strock	228-427	3243	16	27
1973	Rick Popp	70-131	784	7	9
1974	Bruce Arians	53-118	952	3	7
1975	Phil Rogers	25-53	379	3	3
1976	Mitcheal Barnes	39-72	589	5	2
1977	David Lamie	43-107	752	0	10
1978	Steve Casey	61-118	678	2	4
1979	Steve Casey	105-190	1419	10	13
1980	Steve Casey	97-176	1119	13	14
1981	Steve Casey	79-163	1083	4	9
1982	Todd Greenwood	82-148	987	6	7
1983	Mark Cox	86-156	1188	9	7
1984	Mark Cox	86-164	983	5	8
1985	Todd Greenwood	85-169	919	7	9
1986	Erik Chapman	113-222	1627	10	6
1987	Erik Chapman	119-231	1340	10	14
1988	Will Furrer	128-279	1384	6	16
1989	Will Furrer	45-88	589	3	3
1990	Will Furrer	173-296	2122	19	11
1991	Will Furrer	148-257	1820	15	16
1992	Maurice DeShazo	101-215	1504	12	11
1993	Maurice DeShazo	129-230	2080	22	7
1994	Maurice DeShazo	164-296	2110	13	13
1995	Jim Druckenmiller	151-294	2103	14	11

RECEIVING

Year	Player	Rec.	Yds.	TDs
1952	Bob Luttrell	11	142	0
1953	Tom Petty	10	216	0
1954	Tom Petty	9	236	0
1955	Roger Simmons	9	153	0
1956	Carroll Dale	8	157	3
1957	Carroll Dale	17	171	0
1958	Carroll Dale	25	459	6
1959	Carroll Dale	17	408	6
1960	Terry Strock	16	236	6
1961	Terry Strock	10	68	1
1962	Tommy Marvin	11	137	1
1963	Tommy Marvin	28	303	1
1964	Tommy Marvin	21	330	3
1965	Gene Fisher	30	387	2
1966	Ken Barefoot	22	267	4
1967	Ken Barefoot	26	225	2
1968	Danny Cupp	21	323	1
1969	Terry Smoot	18	161	1
1970	Jimmy Quinn	30	481	1
1971	Mike Burnop	46	558	2
1972	Ricky Scales	43	826	7
1973	Ricky Scales	36	772	7
1974	Ricky Scales	34	674	4
1975	Steve Galloway	18	378	4
1976	Moses Foster	20	429	5
1977	Ellis Savage	23	416	0
1978	Dennis Scott	21	300	1
1979	Sidney Snell	43	706	7
1980	Sidney Snell	43	568	8
1981	Mike Giacolone	28	514	7
1982	Mike Giacolone	37	405	2
1983	Mike Shaw	23	357	2
1984	Joe Jones	39	452	1
1985	Donald Snell	31	369	0
1986	Donald Snell	34	661	6
1987	Steve Johnson	38	475	3
1988	Myron Richardson	36	583	1
1989	Myron Richardson	27	450	4
1990	Marcus Mickel	38	409	0
1991	Bo Campbell	29	494	7
1992	Antonio Freeman	32	703	6

1993	Antonio Freeman	32	644	9
1994	Antonio Freeman	38	586	5
1995	Bryan Still	32	628	3

PUNTING

Year	Player	No.	Avg.
1952	Jack Williams	66	40.7
1953	Jack Williams	30	40.9
1954	Tom Petty	40	35.6
1955	Bobby Wolfenden	29	39.9
1956	Bobby Wolfenden	30	37.3
1957	Bobby Conner	25	34.8
1958	Carroll Dale	28	33.6
1959	Carroll Dale	36	32.8
1960	Terry Strock	47	37.2
1961	Terry Strock	35	36.5
1962	Jake Adams	25	38.8
1963	Bob Schweickert	45	39.1
1964	Bob Schweickert	42	37.7
1965	Gene Fisher	49	40.6
1966	Gene Fisher	68	37.9
1967	Gene Fisher	88	37.1
1968	Jack Simcsak	82	38.7
1969	Jack Simcsak	66	41.2
1970	Jack Simcsak	62	38.1
1971	Andy Hromyak	57	39.3
1972	Andy Hromyak	42	41.4
1973	Bruce McDaniel	55	40.3
1974	Bruce McDaniel	53	39.6
1975	Bruce McDaniel	60	37.9
1976	George Roberts	68	41.5
1977	George Roberts	60	42.1
1978	Dave Smigelsky	58	41.0
1979	Dave Smigelsky	58	42.3
1980	Dave Smigelsky	53	39.8
1981	Bill Renner	62	39.5
1982	Bill Renner	79	38.6
1983	David Cox	61	41.0
1984	David Cox	56	41.9
1985	David Cox	55	34.9
1986	Tony Romero	47	36.0
1987	Tony Romero	51	37.9
1988	Kelly Fitzgerald	39	36.7
1989	Chris Baucia	77	37.5
1990	Chris Baucia	66	38.5
1991	Jack Wiltshire	55	37.2
1992	Robbie Colley	57	38.1
1993	Robbie Colley	51	38.4
1994	Robbie Colley	57	42.1
1995	John Thomas	61	38.9

TOTAL OFFENSE

Year	Player	Plays	Yds.
1952	Johnny Dean	208	914
1953	Jack Williams		592
1954	Dickie Beard	131	729
1955	Billy Cranwell	120	593
1956	Jimmy Lugar	156	865
1957	Billy Cranwell	83	407
1958	Billy Holsclaw	230	1227
1959	Alger Pugh	146	859
1960	Warren Price	171	736
1961	Warren Price	186	737
1962	Bob Schweickert	80	513
1963	Bob Schweickert	271	1526
1964	Bob Schweickert	240	1409
1965	Bobby Owens	268	1417
1966	Tommy Stafford	278	1193
1967	Al Kincaid	251	765
1968	Terry Smoot	197	852
1969	Terry Smoot	246	940
1970	Gil Schwabe	159	773

1971	Don Strock	413	2404
1972	Don Strock	480	3170
1973	Phil Rogers	182	1221
1974	Bruce Arians	225	1195
1975	Phil Rogers	264	1141
1976	Roscoe Coles	209	1119
1977	David Lamie	229	1040
1978	Kenny Lewis	184	1020
1979	Steve Casey	295	1622
1980	Steve Casey	248	1287
1981	Cyrus Lawrence	325	1403
1982	Todd Greenwood	227	941
1983	Mark Cox	245	1403
1984	Mark Cox	209	1057
1985	Maurice Williams	167	936
1986	Erik Chapman	308	1583
1987	Erik Chapman	323	1246
1988	Will Furrer	337	1297
1989	Will Furrer	101	590
1990	Will Furrer	329	2046
1991	Will Furrer	280	1849
1992	Maurice DeShazo	315	1710
1993	Maurice DeShazo	313	2177
1994	Maurice DeShazo	379	2081
1995	Jim Druckenmiller	355	2160

SCORING

Year	Player	TDs	PAT/other	FGs	TP
1952	Dickie Beard	5			30
1953	Jack Williams	5			30
1954	Dickie Beard	4	15		39
1955	Don Divers	7			42
	Leo Burke	7			42
1956	Jimmy Lugar	8			48
1957	Barry Frazee	3	13	1	34
1958	Pat Henry	7	1		44
1959	Alger Pugh	11			66
1960	Terry Strock	7			42
1961	Terry Strock	3			18
	Warren Price	3			18
1962	Bob Schweickert	5			30
1963	Sonny Utz	10			60
1964	Sonny Utz	11			66
1965	Bobby Owens	7			42
1966	Tommy Francisco	14			84
1967	Jon Utin	0	17	10	47
1968	Jack Simcsak	0	24	9	51
1969	Terry Smoot	12			72
1970	Perry Tiberio	10			60
1971	James Barber	9			54
1972	James Barber	13			78
1973	Wayne Latimer	0	22	13	61
1974	Bruce Arians	11	1		68
1975	Roscoe Coles	10			60
1976	Roscoe Coles	9	1		56
1977	David Lamie	8			48
1978	Kenny Lewis	10			60
1979	Cyrus Lawrence	9			54
1980	Cyrus Lawrence	8			48
	Sidney Snell	8			48
1981	Don Wade	0	23	13	62
1982	Don Wade	0	14	9	41
1983	Don Wade	0	37	8	61
1984	Don Wade	0	24	12	60
1985	Maurice Williams	9			54
1986	Chris Kinzer	0	27	22	93
1987	Chris Kinzer	0	23	8	47
1988	Chris Kinzer	0	20	12	56
1989	Mickey Thomas	0	14	21	77
1990	Mickey Thomas	0	29	10	59
1991	Tony Kennedy	11			66
1992	Ryan Williams	0	28	12	64

1993		Dwayne Thomas	12				72
1994		Ryan Williams	0	27		17	78
1995		Atle Larsen	0	33		12	69

TACKLING

Yr.	Pos.	Name	TT
1974	lb	Rick Razzano	165
1975	lb	Rick Razzano	177
1976	lb	Rick Razzano	140
1977	lb	Rick Razzano	152
1978	lb	Chip Keatley	102
1979	lb	Chris Cosh	86
1980	lb	Ashley Lee	95
1981	lb	Ashley Lee	146
1982	lb	Mike Johnson	148
1983	lb	Mike Johnson	135
1984	lb	Vince Daniels	113
1985	lb	Paul Nelson	103
1986	lb	Paul Nelson	104
1987	dt	Scott Hill	177
1988	dt	Horacio Moronta	81
1989	ilb	Bobby Martin	79
1990	olb	Archie Hopkins	89
1991	de	Wooster Pack	70
1992	olb	P.J. Preston	89
	ilb	Melendez Byrd	89
1993	lb	Ken Brown	113
1994	lb	George DelRicco	130
1995	lb	George DelRicco	137

TEAM RECORDS

TOTAL OFFENSE, GAME

675	vs. Pittsburgh	9-11-93
641	vs. Maryland	9-25-93
638	vs. Akron	10-14-95
617	vs. William & Mary	10-29-83
605	vs. Houston	10-7-72

TOTAL OFFENSE, SEASON

4885	in 1993	4233	in 1995
4534	in 1983	4182	in 1992
4527	in 1972		

TOTAL PLAYS, GAME

98	vs. Cincinnati	8-31-85
96	vs. Wake Forest	11-22-75
95	vs. South Carolina	11-11-72
94	vs. Richmond	10-26-74
94	vs. Houston	10-7-72
94	vs. N.C. State	9-29-56

TOTAL PLAYS, SEASON

857	in 1972	834	in 1993
853	in 1988	833	in 1982
838	in 1974		

RUSHING ATTEMPTS, GAME

87	vs. Wake Forest	11-22-75
87	vs. South Carolina	10-12-74
86	vs. Richmond	10-26-74
85	vs. N.C. State	9-29-56
81	vs. Virginia	10-27-56

RUSHING ATTEMPTS, SEASON

728	in 1975	649	in 1977
710	in 1976	621	in 1956
704	in 1974		

RUSHING YARDS, GAME

500	vs. Pittsburgh	9-11-93
469	vs. Duke	11-15-69
467	vs. William & Mary	10-12-85
453	vs. Akron	10-14-95
451	vs. William & Mary	10-29-83

RUSHING YARDS, SEASON

3076	in 1975	2932	in 1974
3069	in 1983	2835	in 1956
2992	in 1993		

RUSHING TOUCHDOWNS, GAME

8	vs. Akron	10-14-95
7	vs. VMI	11-24-66
	Pittsburgh	9-11-93
6	on six occasions	
	(most recent: vs. Virginia 11-19-83)	

RUSHING TOUCHDOWNS, SEASON

33	in 1974	27	in 1983
32	in 1956	24	in 1974
28	in 1993		

PASS ATTEMPTS, GAME

53	vs. Houston	10-7-72
51	vs. Cincinnati	8-31-85
50	vs. Oklahoma	9-28-91
49	vs. South Carolina	11-11-72
48	vs. Florida State	9-23-72

PASS ATTEMPTS, SEASON

440	in 1972	324	in 1988
368	in 1971	317	in 1994
329	in 1990		

PASS COMPLETIONS, GAME

34	vs. Houston	10-7-72
31	vs. South Carolina	11-11-72
28	vs. Southern Miss	10-27-90
27	vs. Oklahoma	9-28-91
26	vs. Cincinnati	8-31-85
26	vs. Wake Forest	11-25-72

PASS COMPLETIONS, SEASON

233	in 1972	180	in 1991
202	in 1971	174	in 1994
192	in 1990		

PASSING YARDS, GAME

527	vs. Houston	10-7-72
413	vs. South Carolina	11-11-72
408	vs. Wake Forest	11-25-72
376	vs. Ohio Univ.	10-23-71
355	vs. Oklahoma State	10-14-72

PASSING YARDS, SEASON

3348	in 1972	2214	in 1993
2695	in 1971	2206	in 1995
2373	in 1990		

5	vs. Temple	10-16-93
4	vs. Maryland	9-25-93
4	vs. Ohio Univ.	10-21-72
4	vs. VMI	11-28-68

PASSING TOUCHDOWNS, SEASON

24	in 1993	16	in 1959
20	in 1990	16	in 1991
18	in 1972		

KICKOFF RETURN YARDAGE, GAME

245	vs. South Carolina	10-6-73
240	vs. Alabama	10-27-73
214	vs. Clemson	9-16-89
213	vs. Alabama	11-18-72
206	vs. Maryland	12-2-50

KICKOFF RETURN YARDAGE, SEASON

1431	in 1973	909	in 1987
1075	in 1950	872	in 1988
962	in 1971		

PUNT RETURN YARDAGE, GAME

164	vs. Pittsburgh	10-22-94
154	vs. Richmond	10-21-67
134	vs. Miami	11-4-67
134	vs. Virginia	10-22-60
128	vs. William & Mary	10-28-72
126	vs. West Virginia	10-25-58

PUNT RETURN YARDAGE, SEASON

589	in 1994	537	in 1957
558	in 1952	451	in 1956
554	in 1967		

INTERCEPTIONS, GAME

6	vs. Rutgers	10-31-92
6	vs. Florida State	11-2-68
5	on eight occasions	
	(most recent: vs. South Carolina 10-8-88)	

INTERCEPTIONS, SEASON

27	in 1967	23	in 1954
25	in 1968	22	in 1984
25	in 1968		

INTERCEPTION RETURN YARDAGE, GAME

182	vs. Vanderbilt	11-12-83
151	vs. William & Mary	9-23-67
148	vs. Waynesburg	11-13-54
130	vs. VMI	10-6-84
126	vs. Villanova	11-7-70

INTERCEPTION RETURN YARDAGE, SEASON

594	in 1954	355	in 1983
423	in 1968	350	in 1984
397	in 1967		

INDIVIDUAL RECORDS

TOTAL OFFENSE — PLAYS

Game — 57, Don Strock vs. Houston, 1972
Season — 480, Don Strock, 1972
Career — 1047, Will Furrer, 1988-91

TOTAL OFFENSE — YARDS

Game — 516, Don Strock vs. Houston, 1972
Season — 3170, Don Strock, 1972
Career — 6105, Maurice DeShazo, 1991-94

TOTAL OFFENSE — YARDS PER GAME

Season — 288.2, Don Strock, 1972
Career — 202.4, Don Strock, 1970-72

TOTAL OFFENSE — YARDS PER PLAY

Season — 7.0, Maurice DeShazo, 1993
Career — 6.0, Don Strock, 1970-72

SEASON TOTAL OFFENSE LEADERS

3170	Don Strock , 1972
2404	Don Strock, 1971
2177	Maurice DeShazo, 1993
2160	Jim Druckenmiller, 1995
2081	Maurice DeShazo, 1994
2046	Will Furrer, 1990
1849	Will Furrer, 1991
1710	Maurice DeShazo, 1992
1622	Steve Casey, 1979
1583	Erik Chapman, 1986

CAREER TOTAL OFFENSE LEADERS

Pos.	Name	Yrs.	Plays	Yds.
qb	Maurice DeShazo	1991-94	1026	6105
qb	Don Strock	1970-72	974	5871
qb	Will Furrer	1988-91	1047	5782
qb	Steve Casey	1978-81	982	4987
qb	Mark Cox	1981-85	754	3890
tb	Cyrus Lawrence	1979-82	844	3767
rb	Roscoe Coles	1974-77	658	3458
qb	Bob Schweickert	1962-64	603	3448
rb-qb	Phil Rogers	1973-75	589	3025
tb	Maurice Williams	1983-86	550	2981
qb	Erik Chapman	1985-87	640	2828
tb	Dwayne Thomas	1992-95	576	2696
qb	Todd Greenwood	1982-85	604	2669
tb	Eddie Hunter	1983-86	471	2550
qb	Jim Druckenmiller	1993-	401	2358
tb	Tony Kennedy	1989-92	546	2336
tb	Vaughn Hebron	1989-92	481	2327
tb	Terry Smoot	1967-69	512	2148
rb	James Barber	1971-73	454	2052

RUSHES

Game — 42, Cyrus Lawrence vs. Memphis St., 1981
Season — 325, Cyrus Lawrence, 1981
Career — 843, Cyrus Lawrence, 1979-82

RUSHING, YARDS

Game — 223, Kenny Lewis vs. VMI, 1978
Season — 1403, Cyrus Lawrence, 1981
Career — 3767, Cyrus Lawrence, 1979-82

TOUCHDOWNS SCORED RUSHING

Game — 6, Tommy Francisco vs. VMI, 1966
Season — 13, Tommy Francisco, 1966
           13, James Barber, 1972
Career — 30, Cyrus Lawrence, 1979-82

RUSHING YARDS-PER-CARRY AVERAGE

Season — 6.2, Maurice Williams, 1986
(min. 100 carries)
Career — 5.42, Maurice Williams, 1983-86
(min. 300 carries)

100-YARD RUSHING GAMES

No.	Pos.	Player	Best	Year
16	tb	Cyrus Lawrence	202 vs. Virginia	1981
14	rb	Roscoe Coles	214 vs. Tulsa	1976
11	tb	Eddie Hunter	160 vs. VMI	1984
10	tb	Kenny Lewis	223 vs. VMI	1978
9	rb-qb	Phil Rogers	168 vs. Houston	1975
8	tb	Terry Smoot	171 vs. VMI	1969
8	tb	Maurice Williams	190 vs. Louisville	1985
7	hb	James Barber	164 vs. SMU	1973
7	tb	Vaughn Hebron	165 vs. Bowling Green	1990
7	tb	Dwayne Thomas	172 vs. Rutgers	1994
6	qb	Bob Schweickert	204 vs. Richmond	1963
6	fb	Mickey Fitzgerald	144 vs. West Va.	1977
4	fb	Sonny Utz	146 vs. Tampa	1964
4	tb	Jon Jeffries	160 vs. Cincinnati	1987
4	tb	Tony Kennedy	133 vs. East Carolina	1991
3	tb	Perry Tiberio	170 vs. Duke	1969
3	tb	Tommy Francisco	133 vs. Wake Forest	1965
2	fb	Ken Edwards	197 vs. Florida St.	1968
2	hb	Alger Pugh	129 vs. Wake Forest	1959
2	fb	Paul Adams	113 vs. Virginia	1975
2	tb	Johnnie Edmonds	115 vs. Rhode Island	1980
2	tb	Otis Copeland	132 vs. Wake Forest	1983
2	tb	Desmar Becton	129 vs. Wm. & Mary	1983
2	tb	Ralph Brown	125 vs. Cincinnati	1988
2	tb	Ken Oxendine	135 vs. Akron	1995
1	hb	Dickie Longerbeam	164 vs. Virginia	1965
1	qb	Bobby Owens	158 vs. VMI	1965
1	qb	Mark Cox	125 vs. VMI	1983
1	qb	David Lamie	121 vs. Wm. & Mary	1977
1	tb	Rich Matijevich	119 vs. Wm. & Mary	1969
1	fb	George Constantinides	117 vs. Richmond	1967
1	fb	Earnie Jones	116 vs. Vanderbilt	1985
1	qb	Tommy Stafford	105 vs. Tulane	1966
1	fb	George Heath	104 vs. S. Carolina	1974
1	qb	Steve Casey	101 vs. West Va.	1978
1	fb	Phil Bryant	120 vs. Akron	1991
1	tb	Tommy Edwards	144 vs. Maryland	1993
1	qb	Al Clark	120 vs. Akron	1995

SEASON RUSHING LEADERS

1403	Cyrus Lawrence, 1981
1221	Cyrus Lawrence, 1980
1130	Dwayne Thomas, 1993
1119	Roscoe Coles, 1976
1045	Roscoe Coles, 1975
1036	Phil Rogers, 1973
1029	Maurice Williams, 1986
1020	Kenny Lewis, 1978
940	Terry Smoot, 1969
936	Maurice Williams, 1985

CAREER RUSHING LEADERS

Pos.	Name	Yrs.	No.	Yds.
tb	Cyrus Lawrence	1979-82	843	3767
rb	Roscoe Coles	1974-77	656	3459
tb	Maurice Williams	1983-86	550	2981
tb	Dwayne Thomas	1992-95	576	2696
tb	Eddie Hunter	1983-86	466	2523
rb-qb	Phil Rogers	1973-75	528	2461
tb	Vaughn Hebron	1989-92	481	2327
tb	Tony Kennedy	1989-92	535	2259
tb	Terry Smoot	1967-69	510	2116
rb	James Barber	1971-73	454	2052
fb	Paul Adams	1972-76	470	1984
tb	Kenny Lewis	1976-79	358	1928
qb	Bob Schweickert	1962-64	337	1723
fb	Sonny Utz	1962-64	375	1605
tb	Tommy Francisco	1964-66	366	1555
fb	Mickey Fitzgerald	1976-79	303	1449
hb	Dickie Beard	1953-55	280	1378
tb-rb	Perry Tiberio	1968-70	303	1289

PASSES ATTEMPTED

Game — 53, Don Strock vs. Houston, 1972
Season — 427, Don Strock, 1972
Career — 920, Will Furrer, 1988-91

PASSES COMPLETED

Game — 34, Don Strock vs. Houston, 1972
Season — 228, Don Strock, 1972
Career — 494, Will Furrer, 1988-91

YARDS PASSING

Game — 527, Don Strock vs. Houston, 1972
Season — 3243, Don Strock, 1972
Career — 6009, Don Strock, 1970-72

TOUCHDOWN PASSES THROWN

Game — 4, Don Strock vs. Ohio U., 1972
    4, Maurice DeShazo vs. Maryland, 1993
    4, Maurice DeShazo vs. Temple, 1993
Season — 22, Maurice DeShazo, 1993
Career — 47, Maurice DeShazo, 1991-94

INTERCEPTIONS THROWN

Game — 5, Don Strock vs. Kentucky, 1971
    5, Steve Casey vs. Duke, 1981
    5, Will Furrer vs. N.C. State, 1991
    5, Maurice DeShazo vs. Virginia, 1994
Season — 27, Don Strock, 1972
Career — 47, Don Strock, 1970-72

PASSING, YARDS-PER-GAME AVERAGE

Season — 294.8, Don Strock, 1972
Career — 207.2, Don Strock, 1970-72

PASSING, YARDS-PER-COMPLETION AVERAGE

Season — 16.1, Maurice DeShazo, 1993
Career — 14.4, Maurice DeShazo, 1991-94
    (min. 200 completions)

PASSING, YARDS-PER-ATTEMPT AVERAGE

Season — 9.0, Maurice DeShazo, 1993
    (min. 110 attempts)
Career — 7.7, Maurice DeShazo, 1991-94
    (min. 200 attempts)

PASS COMPLETION PERCENTAGE

Season — .584, Will Furrer, 1990
    (min. 110 attempts)
Career — .542, Mark Cox, 1981-85
    (min. 200 attempts)

SEASON PASSING LEADERS

3243	Don Strock, 1972
2577	Don Strock, 1971
2122	Will Furrer, 1990
2110	Maurice DeShazo, 1994
2103	Jim Druckenmiller, 1995
2080	Maurice DeShazo, 1993
1820	Will Furrer, 1991
1627	Erik Chapman, 1986
1504	Maurice DeShazo, 1992
1419	Steve Casey, 1979

CAREER PASSING LEADERS

Name	Yrs.	Comp-Att.	TDs	Yds.
Don Strock	1970-72	440-829	29	6009
Will Furrer	1988-91	494-920	43	5915
Maurice DeShazo	1991-94	397-745	47	5720
Steve Casey	1978-81	342-647	29	4299
Mark Cox	1981-85	281-518	22	3526
Erik Chapman	1985-87	234-458	20	2996
Todd Greenwood	1982-85	234-443	16	2721
Jim Druckenmiller	1993-	171-332	17	2312

Name	Yrs.	Comp-Att.	TDs	Yds.
Bob Schweickert	1962-64	133-266	18	1725
David Lamie	1975-78	79-190	4	1327
Bruce Arians	1972-74	78-174	6	1270
Billy Holsclaw	1956-58	87-169	11	1262
Johnny Dean	1952-54	93-206	2	1243
Al Kincaid	1967-69	122-261	5	1202

PASSES CAUGHT

Game — 13, Donald Snell vs. Cincinnati, 1985
    13, Nick Cullen vs. So. Miss., 1990
Season — 46, Mike Burnop, 1971
Career — 121, Antonio Freeman, 1991-94

YARDS GAINED BY RECEIVING

Game — 213, Ricky Scales vs. Wake Forest, 1972
Season — 826, Ricky Scales, 1972
Career — 2272, Ricky Scales, 1972-74

TOUCHDOWN RECEPTIONS

Game — 3, Ricky Scales vs. Ohio U., 1972
    3, Antonio Freeman vs. Temple, 1993
Season — 9, Antonio Freeman , 1993
Career — 22, Antonio Freeman, 1991-94

BEST AVERAGE PER CATCH

Season — 22.0, Antonio Freeman, 1992
    22.0, Moses Foster, 1976
    (min. 20 catches)

SEASON RECEIVING LEADERS

826	Ricky Scales, 1972
772	Ricky Scales, 1973
706	Sidney Snell, 1979
705	Donnie Reel, 1971
703	Antonio Freeman, 1992
674	Ricky Scales, 1974
661	Donald Snell, 1986
644	Antonio Freeman, 1993
628	Bryan Still, 1995
586	Antonio Freeman, 1994
583	Myron Richardson, 1988

CAREER PASS RECEIVING LEADERS

Pos.	Name	Yrs.	Rec	TDs	Yds.
se	Antonio Freeman	1991-94	121	22	2207
wr	Ricky Scales	1972-74	113	18	2272
se	Mike Giacolone	1979-82	103	10	1384
se	Myron Richardson	1986-89	100	9	1541
se	Donald Snell	1983-86	92	7	1409
te	Mike Burnop	1970-72	90	5	1141
wb	Sidney Snell	1978-80	86	15	1274
te	Steve Johnson	1984-87	84	8	1058
flk	Marcus Mickel	1988-91	77	1	868
flk	Bryan Still	1992-95	74	11	1458
se-wb	Jimmy Quinn	1969-71	72	4	1262
se	Nick Cullen	1987-90	70	5	946
wr	Donnie Reel	1970-72	68	5	1260
te	Ken Barefoot	1965-67	68	8	752
se	Bo Campbell	1989-92	68	9	1145
se	Carroll Dale	1956-59	67	15	1195
se	Jermaine Holmes	1992-95	67	7	993
flk	Steve Sanders	1990-93	60	5	960
te	Mike Shaw	1980-83	60	7	904
e	Tommy Marvin	1962-64	60	5	770
tb	Vaughn Hebron	1989-92	60	4	596
rb	J.B. Barber	1971-73	58	1	484
wb-te	Terrence Howell	1982-85	55	6	717
se	Gene Fisher	1965-67	55	3	698

CAREER SCORING LEADERS

Pos.	Name	Yrs.	TDs	PAT	/other	FGs	TP
pk	Ryan Williams	1991-94	0	137		39	254
pk	Chris Kinzer	1985-88	0	93		47	234
pk	Don Wade	1981-84	0	98		42	224
rb	James Barber	1971-73	30				180
tb	Cyrus Lawrence	1979-82	30				180
rb	Roscoe Coles	1974-77	29		1		176
tb	Tony Kennedy	1989-92	26		1		158
tb	Maurice Williams	1983-86	25				150
tb	Dwayne Thomas	1992-95	25				150
pk	Wayne Latimer	1973-75	0	72		25	147
tb	Terry Smoot	1967-69	24				144
pk	Mickey Thomas	1989-91	0	44		31	137
qb	Bob Schweickert	1962-64	22		1		134
tb	Tommy Francisco	1964-66	22		1		134
fb	Sonny Utz	1962-64	22				132
tb	Eddie Hunter	1983-86	22				132
pk	Jon Utin	1965-67	0	63		20	123
pk	Jack Simcsak	1968-70	0	59		21	122
hb	Dickie Beard	1952-55	12	43		1	118
wr	Ricky Scales	1972-74	19		1		116
pk	Dave Strock	1971-72	0	50		22	116

PUNT RETURNS

Game — 10, John Ludlow vs. Virginia, 1982
      10, Bo Campbell vs. Akron, 1989
Season — 51, John Ludlow, 1982
Career — 136, John Ludlow, 1979-82

YARDAGE ON PUNT RETURNS

Game — 164, Antonio Freeman vs. Pitt, 1994
Season — 467, Antonio Freeman, 1994
Career — 837, John Ludlow, 1979-82

TDS ON PUNT RETURNS

Game — 1, shared by many
Season — 3, Frank Loria, 1966
Career — 4, Frank Loria, 1965-67

PUNT RETURN AVERAGE

Season — 18.2, Bo Campbell, 1991
    (15 or more returns)
Career — 13.3, Frank Loria, 1965-67

PUNT RETURNS, TEAM

Game — 10, vs. VMI, 1971
      10, vs. Virginia, 1982
      10, vs. Clemson, 1989
Season — 53, 1982

YARDAGE ON PUNT RETURNS, TEAM

Game — 164, vs. Pittsburgh, 1994
Season — 589, 1994

TDS ON PUNT RETURNS, TEAM

Season — 3, 1966

PUNT RETURN AVERAGE, TEAM

Season — 17.1, (35 returns) 1957

KICKOFF RETURNS

Game — 9, James Barber vs. Tulsa, 1971
     9, Billy Hardee vs. Alabama, 1973
Season — 33, Billy Hardee, 1973
Career — 67, Jon Jeffries, 1987-91

YARDAGE ON KICKOFF RETURNS

Game — 214, Marcus Mickel vs. Clemson, 1989
Season — 758, Billy Hardee, 1973
Career — 1447, Jon Jeffries, 1987-91

TDS ON KICKOFF RETURNS

Season — 1, shared by many
Career — 2, Terry Strock, 1959-61

KICKOFF RETURN AVERAGE

Season — 34.3, Tommy Francisco, 1965
    (10 or more returns)
Career — 24.8, Dickie Longerbeam, 1965-68

KICKOFF RETURNS, TEAM

Game — 12, vs. Alabama, 1973
Season — 67, 1950

YARDAGE ON KICKOFF RETURNS, TEAM

Game — 245, vs. South Carolina, 1973
Season — 1431, 1973

TDS ON KICKOFF RETURNS, TEAM

Season — 2, 1965

KICKOFF RETURN AVERAGE, TEAM

Season — 27.4, 1965

TACKLES.

Game — 30, Rick Razzano vs. Kentucky, 1977
Season — 177, Rick Razzano, 1975
       177, Scott Hill, 1987
Career — 634, Rick Razzano, 1974-77

UNASSISTED TACKLES

Game — 21, Rick Razzano vs. Richmond, 1975
Season — 102, Rick Razzano, 1975
Career — 368, Rick Razzano, 1974-77

ASSISTED TACKLES

Game — 15, Ashley Lee vs. Richmond, 1981
      15, Mike Johnson vs. Miami (Fla.), 1982
Season — 110, Scott Hill, 1987
Career — 266, Rick Razzano, 1974-77

QUARTERBACK SACKS

Game — 4, Bruce Smith vs. Duke, 1983
     4, Bruce Smith vs. Wm. & Mary, 1984
     4, Morgan Roane vs. Wm. & Mary, 1985
Season — 22, Bruce Smith, 1983
Career — 46, Bruce Smith, 1981-84

Season — 31, Bruce Smith, 1983
Career — 71, Bruce Smith, 1981-84

INTERCEPTIONS

Game — 3, Ron Davidson vs. Florida St., 1967
3, Lenny Smith vs. Wake Forest, 1968
3, John Bell vs. Florida St., 1973
3, John Bell vs. West Va., 1974
3, Paul Davis vs. Florida St., 1979
3, Derek Carter vs. VMI, 1982
Season — 9, Ron Davidson, 1967
Career — 18, Gene Bunn, 1976-78

YARDS GAINED ON INTERCEPTION

Game — *182, fs Ashley Lee vs. Vanderbilt, 1983
Season — 210, hb Johnny Watkins, 1960
Career — 351, fs Ashley Lee, 1980-84

TOUCHDOWNS ON INTERCEPTION

Game — 2, Don Divers vs. VMI, 1954
2, Ashley Lee vs. Vanderbilt, 1983
Season — 2, Don Divers, 1954
2, Mike Widger, 1968
2, Ashley Lee, 1983
Career — 3, Don Divers, 1954-56
3, Mike Widger, 1967-69

*NCAA record

TOP 25 FINISHES

ASSOCIATED PRESS

1995: No. 10	1986: No. 20
1954: No. 16	1993: No. 22

COACHES' POLL

1995: No. 9	1993: No. 20
1986: No. 20	1994: No. 24

UNITED PRESS INTERNATIONAL

1995: No. 9	1993: No. 21
1966: No. 20	1994: No. 24

BOWL RESULTS

1995 NOKIA SUGAR BOWL

Virginia Tech 28, Texas 10

Virginia Tech	0	7	7	14	—	28
Texas	7	3	0	0	—	10

TEX (4:32 1st) — Fitzgerald 4 pass from Brown (Dawson kick)
TEX (13:19 2nd) — FG Dawson 52
VT (2:34 2nd) — Still 60 punt return (Larsen kick)
VT (2:32 3rd) — Parker 2 run (Larsen kick)
VT (12:28 4th) — Still 54 pass from Druckenmiller (Larsen kick)
VT (5:06 4th) — Baron 20 fumble return (Larsen kick)

Team Stats	VT	TEX
First downs	20	15
Rushes-yds.	32-105	33-78
Passing yds.	266	148
Return yds.	84	42
Passes	18-34-1	14-37-3
Punts-avg.	8-37	9-40
Fumbles-lost	5-2	2-1
Penalties-yds.	11-99	9-91
Time of poss.	30:25	29:35
Sacks by	5-36	2-1

Individual Leaders

Rushing — VT, D. Thomas 15-62, Oxendine 8-31, Edmonds 3-10, Parker 2-4, Druckenmiller 3-1, Whipple 1-(-3); TEX, Williams 12-62, Mitchell 15-59, Brown 6-(-43).
Passing — VT, Druckenmiller 18-34-1-266; TEX, Brown 14-36-3-148, McLemore 0-1-0-0.
Receiving — VT, Still 6-119, Jennings 6-77, Holmes 2-30, Edmonds 2-16, White 1-16, Parker 1-8; TEX, M. Adams 6-92, Fitzgerald 3-21, Davis 2-27, Williams 1-6, McGarity 1-1, Mitchell 1-1.

1994 GATOR BOWL

Tennessee 45, Virginia Tech 23

Tennessee	14	21	0	10	—	45
Virginia Tech	0	10	6	7	—	23

UT — J. Stewart 1 run (Becksvoort kick)
UT — Nash 36 pass from Manning (Becksvoort kick)
UT — Graham 2 run (Becksvoort kick)
VT — D. Thomas 1 run (Williams kick)
UT — J. Stewart 1 run (Becksvoort kick)
UT — Jones 20 pass from J. Stewart (Becksvoort kick)
VT — FG Williams 30
VT — DeShazo 7 run (Williams kick)
UT — J. Stewart 5 run (Becksvoort kick)
UT — FG Becksvoort 19
VT — Still 9 pass from Druckenmiller (Williams kick)

Team Stats	VT	UT
First downs	22	18
Rushes-yds.	43-189	47-245
Passing yds.	237	250
Return yds.	18	112
Passes	23-38-2	16-23-0
Punts-avg.	5-43.0	5-43.0
Fumbles-lost	5-1	0-0
Penalties-yds.	3-25	7-58
Time of poss.	29:05	30:55

Individual Statistics

Rushing — VT, D. Thomas 19-102, DeShazo 11-39, Edmonds 5-29, Still 1-8, Oxendine 4-7, Parker 1-3, Edwards 1-1, Druckenmiller 1-0; UT, J. Stewart 22-87, Jones 1-76, B. Stewart 2-31, Manning 2-29, Graham 8-30, Pilow 5-4, Phillips 2-3, Nash 1-1, Ford 2-1, Kerney 1-0, Wheaton 1-(-13).
Passing — VT, DeShazo 17-30-2-140, Druckenmiller 6-8-0-97; UT, Manning 12-19-0-189, B. Stewart 3-3-0-42, J. Stewart 1-1-0-19.
Receiving — VT, Still 5-79, Holmes 5-45, Freeman 4-30, D. THomas 3-18, Oxendine 2-13, Martin 2-6, Jennings 1-41, Scales 1-5; UT, Kent 6-116, Nash

3-54, Jones 2-37, Phillips 1-14, Silvan
1-10, Horn 1-8, J. Stewart 1-7, Staley 1-4.

1993 INDEPENDENCE BOWL

Virginia Tech 45, Indiana 20

Virginia Tech	7	21	0	17	—	45
Indiana	7	6	0	7	—	20

IU (5:36 1st) — Lewis 75 pass from Paci
(Manolopoulos kick)
VT (0:09 1st) — D. Thomas 13 pass from DeShazo
(Williams kick)
VT (11:14 2nd) — Swarm 6 run (Williams kick)
IU (8:47 2nd) — FG Manolopoulos 26
IU (5:25 2nd) — FG Manolopoulos 40
VT (0:23 2nd) — Lewis 20 fumble return (Williams
kick)
VT (0:00 2nd) — Banks 80 blocked FG return
(Williams kick)
VT (9:37 4th) — Freeman 42 pass from DeShazo
(Williams kick)
VT (9:21 4th) — Edwards 5 run (Williams kick)
VT (6:00 4th) — FG Williams 42
IU (4:26 4th) — Lewis 42 pass from Dittoe
(Manolopoulos kick)

Team Stats	VT	IU
First downs	17	11
Rushes-yds.	48-125	31-20
Passing yds.	193	276
Return yds.	38	61
Passes	19-33-2	17-37-2
Punts-avg.	8-39.0	7-38.0
Fumbles-lost	2-1	2-2
Penalties-yds.	8-84	7-55
Time of poss.	32:48	27:12
Sacks by	7-42	2-12

Individual Statistics
Rushing — VT, Thomas 24-65, Swarm 9-40,
Edwards 5-15, R. White 4-3, DeShazo 5-1,
Druckenmiller 101; IU, Thurman 1-37, Chaney,
11-34, Batts 3-10, Glover 3-6, Thomas 1-(-4), Paci
5-(-26), Dittoe 7-(-37).
Passing — VT, DeShazo 19-33-2-193; IU, Paci
10-22-1-171, Dittoe 7-14-1-105, DiGuilio 0-1-0-0.
Receiving — VT, Freeman 5-66, Thomas 4-27, Burke
3-26, C. White 2-35, Sanders 2-15, Swarm
1-13, Edmonds 1-6, Still 1-5; IU, Lewis 6-177, Hales
2-49, Matthews 2-35, Glover 2-1, Chaney 2-(-1),
Baety 1-9, Hobbs 1-4, Eggebrecht 1-2.

1986 PEACH BOWL

Virginia Tech 25, N.C. State 24

Virginia Tech	10	0	6	9	—	25
N.C. State	7	14	0	3	—	24

VT (11:04 1st) — Hunter 1 run (Kinzer kick)
NCSU (6:41 1st) — Bulluck recover blocked-punt in
end zone (Cofer kick)
VT (1:06 1st) — FG Kinzer 46
NCSU (8:55 2nd) — Worthen 25 pass from Kramer
(Cofer kick)
NCSU (4:31 2nd) — Britt 5 pass from Kramer (Cofer
kick)
VT (0:33 3rd) — Williams 1 run (Pass failed)
VT (9:36 4th) — Johnson 6 pass from Chapman
(Run failed)
NCSU (7:12 4th) — FG Cofer 33
VT (0:00 4th) — FG Kinzer 40

Team Stats	VT	NCSU
First downs	29	16
Rushes-yds.	60-287	37-132
Passing yds.	200	155
Return yds.	14	15

Passes	30-20-2	19-12-0
Punts-avg.	2-34.0	5-42.8
Fumbles-lost	1-1	2-2
Penalties-yds.	5-51	0-3-25
Time of poss.	36:06	23:54

Individual Statistics
Rushing — VT, Williams 16-129, Hunter 22-113,
Jones 7-32, Donnelly 3-10, Everrett 1-6, Chapman
11-(-3); NCSU, Crite 14-101, Crumpler 9-21,
Hollodick 1-5, Kramer 10-4, Harris 4-1.
Passing — VT, Chapman 30-20-2 200; NCSU,
Kramer 19-12-0 155.
Receiving — VT, Johnson, S 6-54, Williams, M 4-39,
Snell 4-37, Hunter 2-34, Donnelly 2-19, Everett 1-12,
Richardson 1-5, NCSU, Worthen 5-70, Jeffiries 3-44,
Crumpler 2-27, Harris, F. 1-9, Britt 1-5.

1984 INDEPENDENCE BOWL

Virginia Tech 7, Air Force 23

Virginia Tech	7	0	0	0	—	7
Air Force	3	7	0	13	—	23

AF (5:43 1st) — FG Mateos 35
VT (4:23 1st) — Williams 3 run (Wade kick)
AF (8:50 2nd) — Simmons 3 run (Mateos kick)
AF (6:00 4th) — Brown 2 run (Mateos kick)
AF (2:08 4th) — Weiss 13 run (Mateos kick)

Team Stats	VT	AF
First downs	15	17
Rushes-yds.	42-207	55-221
Passing yds.	102	49
Return yds.	31	17
Passes	26-11-2	7-6-0
Punts-avg.	4-40.0	6-42.5
Fumbles-lost	2-2	2-0
Penalties-yds.	11-112	4-30
Time of poss.	25:52	34:08
Sacks by	3-11	3-16

Individual Statistics
Rushing — VT, Hunter 12 -75, Williams 12-60, Cox,
M. 10-33, Bowe 4-23, Becton 3-18, Greenwood 1-(-
2); AF, Weiss 29-93, Evans 15-58, Simmons 5-27,
Pittman 1-24, Brown 3-8, Knorr 1-6.
Passing —VT, Cox, M. 17-6-1 50, Greenwood 8-5-0
52, Hunter 1-0-1; AF, Weiss 7-6-0 49.
Receiving — VT, Rider 4-45, Nelson 3-24, Jones 2-21,
Howell 1-7, Bowe 1-5; AF, Coleman 1-16, Fleming 1-
14, Brennan 1-9, Simmons 2-7, Brown 1-3.

1980 PEACH BOWL

Miami 20, Virginia Tech 10

Miami	7	7	3	3	—	20
Virginia Tech	0	3	7	0	—	10

UM (12:37 1st) — Brodsky 15 pass from Kelly
(Miller kick)
UM (13:47 2nd) — Hobbs 12 run (Miller kick)
VT (0:29 2nd) — 42 Laury FG
VT (8:52 3rd) — Lawrence 1 run (Laury kick)
UM (0:29 3rd) — 31 Miller FG
UM (6:27 4th) — 37 Miller FG

Team Stats	UM	VT
First downs	19	19
Rushes-yds.	42-163	50-180
Passing yds.	179	119
Return yds.	13	2
Passes	22-11-1	24-9-2
Punts-avg.	5-37.0	6-38.1
Fumbles-lost	4-1	3-0
Penalties-yds.	6-66	7-72
Time of poss.	29:14	20:25

Individual Statistics
Rushing — UM, Roan 16-86, Hobbs 10-66, Neal

5-12, Rush 2-5, Joiner 2-1, Griffin 2-5, Kelly 5-(-21); VT, Lawrence 27-134, Dovel 9-41, Casey 13-8, Paige 1-(-3).
Passing — UM, Kelly 22-11-1; VT, Casey 23-9-1, Lawrence 1-0-1.
Receiving — UM, Brodsky 4-80, Baratta 2-34, Belk 1-27, Walker 2-26, Rodriguez 1-7, Hobbs 1-5; VT, Purdham 2-56, Giacalone 2-30, Hite 2-15, KcKee 1-8, Snell 1-8, Donel 1-2.

1968 LIBERTY BOWL

Mississippi 34, Virginia Tech 17

Virginia Tech	17	0	0	0	–	17
Mississippi	0	14	7	13	–	34

VT (14:23 1st) — Edwards 58 run (Simcsak kick)
VT (12:43 1st) — Smoot 74 run (Simcsak kick)
VT (1:49 1st) — FG Simcsak 29
MISS (14:30 2nd) — Shows 21 pass from Manning (Brown kick)
MISS (4:28 2nd) — Felts 23 pass from Manning (Brown kick)
MISS (14:41 3rd) — Hindman 79 run (Brown kick)
MISS (11:58 4th) — Baily 70 interception return (Brown kick)
MISS (9:09 4th) — FG Brown 46
MISS (0:00 4th) — FG Brown 26

Team Stats	MISS	VT
First downs	15	16
Rushes-yds.	46-185	60-330
Passing yds.	141	2
Return yds.	109	36
Passes	28-12-1	7-1-2
Punts-avg.	5-37.4	7-40.8
Fumbles-lost	3-2	5-3
Penalties-yds.	4-30	12-120

Individual Statistics
Rushing — VT, Edwards 12-119, Smoot 21-91, Kincaid 15-55, Constantinedes 4-45, Humphries 5-8, Longerbean 1-7, Tiberio 2-5; MISS, Hindman 15-121, Bowen 19-65, Felts 1-0, Manning 11-(-1).
Passing — VT, Humphries 1-3-0-2, Kincaid 0-4-0-0; MISS, Manning 12-28-0-141.
Receiving — VT, Crigger 1-2; MISS, Shows 6-70, Hindman 3-32, Felts 1-23, Bowen 1-8, Franks 1-8.

1966 LIBERTY BOWL

Miami 14, Virginia Tech 7

Miami	0	0	0	7	—	14
Virginia Tech	7	0	0	0	—	7

VT (7:34 1st) — Fransisco 1 run (Utin kick)
UM (4:20 3rd) — Mira 7 pass from Miller (Harris kick)
UM (8:05 4th) — McGee 1 run (Harris kick)

Team Stats	UM	VT
First downs	11	7
Rushes-yds.	44-55	40-36
Passing yds.	108	75
Return yds.	44	7
Passes	10-28	6-16
Punts-avg.	8-30.1	11-39.3
Fumbles-lost	1	2
Penalties-yds.	7-80	6-57

Individual Statistics
Rushing — UM, Miller 11-(-24), Acuff 6-25, McGee 12-36, Mira 11-9, McGuirt 1-1, Cassidy 2-4, Domke 1-4; VT, Stafford 8-(-16), Pilano 4-10, Barcia 3-15, Francisco 21-55, Barker 3-(-16), Beamer 1-(-12).
Passing — UM, Miller 26-9-0, Olivo 2-1-0; VT, Stafford 13-4-1, Barker 3-2-0.
Receiving — UM, Smith 1-2, Russo 2-15, Cox 5-77, Mira 2-14; VT, Barefoot 4-34, Cupp 1-35, Pilano 1-6.

1946 SUN BOWL

Cincinnati 18, Virginia Tech 7

Cincinnati	0	0	12	6	—	18
Virginia Tech	0	0	0	6	—	6

Team Stats	Cin	VT
First downs	16	11
Rushes-yds.	369	34
Passing yds.	94	85
Return yds.	109	64
Passes	5-18	4-15
Punts-avg.	19.0	41.0
Fumbles-lost	0	0
Penalty yds.	85	25

Scoring summary and individual leaders are not available.

LETTERMEN

A Abraham, Jack 1969-71; Adams, Jim 1946-47; Adams, Jake 1961-63; Adams, Paul 1972, 74-76; Agee, Peery 1983-84; Agemy, Jamel 1984-87; Aguilar, Art 1968; Albright, Kyle 1961-63; Albrittain, Chris 1977-78; Alexander, Kirk 1989-92; Allen, Bob 1952-53; Allen, Bobby 1979-81; Ambers, Andy 1984-86; Amos, Mike 1988; Anderson, Van 1939-41; Anderson, Billy 1952-54; Anderson, Lars 1980; Arbaugh, Mike 1973-74, 76; Arians, Bruce 1972-74; Arrington, Marvin 1990-92; Arthur, Richard 1973; Ashworth, Fred 1942; Ausbrooks, Dwight 1983-85.

B Babb, Billy 1962-63; Babione, Dale 1975-77; Bailey, Corbin 1956-57; Bailey, Darryl 1962-64; Bailey, Dave 1968-70; Bailey, Jeff 1977-80; Bailey, Leslie 1986-89; Bailey, Ricky 1983; Ballance, Jeff 1984-86; Ballard, Frank 1945-47; Banks, Antonio 1993-95; Banks, Jim 1976; Banks, Mac 1934-36; Barber, J.B. 1971-73; Barbour, Billy 1942, 46-47; Barefoot, Ken 1965-67; Barefoot, Ken Jr. 1987-88; Barile, Ray 1959-61; Barnes, Mitcheal 1974-76; Barnette, Clyde 1958; Barns, Clinton 1945; Baron, Jim 1994-95; Barry, Chris 1990-93; Barton, Bill 1968; Bartrug, Ed 1957-59; Basham, Bernard 1990-93; Bass, Trenton 1992-94; Baucia, Chris 1988-90; Beamer, Frank 1966-68; Beard, Dickie 1952-55; Beard, Ralph 1945-46, 48-49; Bearekman, Larry 1972-74; Beasley, Roy 1946-48; Beasley, Tom 1973-76; Becton, Desmar 1983-85;

Behl, Dennis 1980; Belcher, A.H. 1940, 42; Belcher, Gippy 1976-78; Belcher, J.R. 1937-38; Bell, John 1972-74; Bennett, Bill 1949; Bennett, Kevin 1989; Berish, Jason 1995; Bertovich, Tony 1971; Bianchin, Mike 1993-95; Bigelow, Jud 1964, 67; Birtsch, Greg 1974, 76-78; Blackburn, Preston 1967-69; Blacken, Malcolm 1985-88; Blackmon, Tony 1979; Blandford, Mason 1941-42; Blankenship, Bo 1985-86; Blankenship, Charlie 1959; Bledsoe, Brent 1973-74; Bloomer, Joe 1962, 64; Blueford, Morris 1973-75; Blunt, Larry 1973-76; Boatwright, William 1988-91; Bobbitte, Gerald 1961-62; Bocko, Steve 1967-69; Boitnott, Tim 1987-89; Bolton, Jeff 1979-81; Bond, Bob 1971; Booth, Don 1952-53; Booth, Jack 1973; Borden, Karl 1987-90; Borden, Mike 1979-80; Bosiack, Tim 1969-71; Boswell, I.W. 1939; Botnick, Benny 1932, 34; Bowe, Nigel 1982-84; Bowen, Rich 1995; Bowles, Floyd Jr. 1945-47; Bowling, Andy 1964-66; Bowling, Herb 1961; Boyle, Dean 1950-51; Bradley, Frank 1951; Bradley, Henry 1974-77; Bradley, Nate 1987; Bradshaw, Bill 1935; Brammer, Mike 1974; Branch, Tyrone 1984; Breen, Gene 1961-63; Breheny, Chris 1992-93; Bria, Sammy 1969-71; Brilliant, Ricky 1979; Brinkley, Ed 1956-58; Briscoe, Mark 1987-88; Britts, Bill 1979; Brooks, Greg 1982-85; Brown, Cornell 1993-95; Brown, Frank 1952-55; Brown, Geoff 1980-82; Brown, Glenn 1972; Brown, Ken 1991-94; Brown, Ralph

Chapter 8: By the Numbers **155**

1987-88, 90; Brown, Robert 1980-81; Brown, Roger 1986-89; Brown, Todd 1989-90; Brown, Wilson 1935-36; Browne, Wally 1979-82; Brownell, Jud 1967-68; Bruce, Donnie 1964-66; Bruce, George 1987; Bruce, Maynard 1946-47; Bryant, Phil 1988-91; Bryant, Tommy 1951; Bryson, Jimmy 1989-90; Buchanan, G.S. 1939; Bulheller, Eddie 1964-66; Bunn, Gene 1976-78; Burke, John 1990-93; Burke, Leo 1952-55; Burks, Jim 1956-58; Burleigh, Bryan 1982-84; Burleson, Hayes 1954-55; Burnette, Gene 1950; Burnop, Mike 1970-72; Burns, Tommy 1945-46, 48; Bush, Rickey 1974; Buskirk, Blair 1974-76; Byrd, Ken 1957-59; Byrd, Melendez 1989-92.

C Cahill, Mike 1962-63; Callison, Mike 1975; Camaioni, Alex 1962-63; Cameron, Archie 1937-38; Camp, Cass 1979-81; Camp, Don 1954; Campbell, Bo 1989-92; Campbell, Bryan 1988-91; Campbell, Johnny 1950; Cannaday, Mike 1980-81; Cannon, Steve 1975-76; Capps, Larry 1974-76; Carpenito, Pat 1955-57; Carpenito, Tommy 1970-72; Carpenter, Buck 1934-35; Carpenter, Keion 1995; Carter, Derek 1981-84; Carter, Eddie 1967-68; Cartwright, Matt 1970; Cartwright, Pete 1962; Cary, Phil 1962-63; Casey, Al 1932-33; Casey, Rickie 1975; Casey, Steve 1978-81; Casto, Ron 1948-50; Chambers, Coy 1946-47, 49; Chamblee, Al 1987-90; Chapman, Erik 1986-87; Charlton, Leroy 1992, 94; Chasen, Irvin 1941-42; Chung, Eugene 1988-91; Church, Joe 1948-50; Churchill, Bob 1962, 64; Clapp, Mike 1986; Clark, Al 1995; Clark, Daniel 1942; Clark, Gerald 1939-41; Clarke, Jake 1980-83; Cobb, Freddie 1966; Cockrell, Randy 1986-89; Cogan, Dennis 1971; Coleman, Hank 1992-95; Coleman, Jim 1938-40; Coleman, Rainer 1984-85; Coles, Roscoe 1974-77; Colley, Robbie 1992-94; Collis, Chris 1969; Collum, Pete 1947-49; Colobro, Nick 1970-72; Comer, Glen 1977; Conaty, Billy 1993-95; Conlin, Jon 1970; Connor, Bobby 1955-57; Constantinides, George 1966-68; Cook, Rusty 1983; Cooke, Donnie 1969-70; Cooke, Jack 1946-47; Cooper, Tom 1974-76; Copeland, Otis 1982-83; Copenhaver, Jim 1933-34; Cosh, Chris 1977-79; Cothran, Bo 1987-88; Courtney, Chris 1973; Cowan, Howard 1950; Cowne, John 1980-83; Cox, David 1983-85; Cox, Joe 1962; Cox, Rod 1969-70; Cox, Mark 1982-85; Cox, Mike 1992; Coyner, Doug 1971; Crabtree, Bob 1959-60; Cramer, Bryson 1977; Cranwell, Billy 1954-55, 57; Cranwell, Dickie 1963-64; Creasey, Skip 1973-74; Creekmore, Larry 1967-69; Cregger, Doug 1952-53; Cregger, Pete 1935-37; Crigger, Dee 1967-69; Crittenden, Ray 1992; Cruickshank, Bobby 1954-56; Cruise, Scott 1983-85; Cuba, Chuck 1954-55; Culicerto, Phil 1982; Cullen, Nick 1987-90; Culpepper, Clarence 1965-67; Cupp, Danny 1966, 68; Cure, Allen 1974-75.

D Dabbs, Bobby 1971-72; Dahl, Jeff 1979-81; Dale, Carroll 1956-59; Daley, Bill 1954-56; Dalzell, Tom 1954, 56; Daniels, Greg 1988-91; Daniels, Sam 1992; Daniels, Vince 1984; Darnell, W.T. 1937; Davidson, Bloice 1958-59, 61; Davidson, Ron 1966-68; Davie, Jim 1983-86; Davis, Don 1990-92; Davis, Ernie 1986-89; Davis, George 1949; Davis, Junior 1936-37; Davis, Paul 1979-80; Davis, Robert 1990; Davis, Ron 1973-75; Davis, Rondal 1974-76; Davis, William 1941-42; Dawson, Scott 1966-67; Dawyot, Pete 1967-69; Dean, Johnny 1951-54; Dedo, Damon 1965-67; DeHart, David 1975-77; DelRicco, George 1992-95; DelViscio, Nick 1968-70; DeMarr, Buddy 1970-71; DeMuro, Phil 1937-39; Denardo, Bruce 1970; Denardo, Pat 1947-48; DePoy, James 1990-92; DeShazo, Dick 1946-47; DeShazo, Maurice 1992-94; Devlin, W.H. 1937-38; Dick, Kevin 1973-75; Dickerson, Herman 1934-36; DiNapoli, Gennaro 1994-95; Divers, Don 1954-56; Dobbins, John 1970-72; Dodge, Ben 1934-35; Dodson, Dennis 1971-73; Dodson, George 1973; Dolphin, Dave 1975-76, 78; Donnelly, Sean 1985-87; Dotson, William 1990-91; Doty, Jeff 1991; Dove, Mitch 1986, 88; Dovel, Scott 1978-81; Doxey, Lloyd 1935-37; Dozier, Vernon 1993-94; Drakeford, Tyronne 1990-93; Drew, Greg 1986-87; Drinkard, John 1977-79; Druckenmiller, Jim 1993-95; Dudley, Tim 1985; Dutton, Howard 1947-49.

E Eakin, Lowell 1980; Eastman, Frank 1957, 59; Ebert, Dave 1954-56; Eddy, Danny 1987-89; Edmond, Tyron 1995; Edmonds, Brian 1993-95; Edmonds, Johnnie 1980; Edwards, Billy 1963-65; Edwards, Danny 1995; Edwards, Ken 1967-69; Edwards, Lacy 1962-64; Edwards, Randall 1961; Edwards, Tommy 1993-94; Ellenbogen, Bill 1971-72; Ellison, M.L. 1938-39; Ellsworth, Steve 1983-86; England, Ray 1955-57; Engle, Paul 1976-78; English, Red 1932-33; Evans, George 1979-82; Everett, David 1985-87.

F Fallen, Larry 1977-78; Farmer, Dave 1965-66; Farmer, John 1961; Farr, Jim 1958-60; Faulkner Mike 1975-76, 78-79; Ferrell, William 1992-94; Fisher, Bud 1948-50; Fisher, Gene 1965-67; Fittro, Louis 1934-35; Fitts, Ray 1982-85; Fitzgerald, John 1980-82; Fitzgerald, Kelly 1989; Fitzgerald, Mickey 1976-79; FitzHugh, John 1985-87; Fixx, Jimmy 1938; Fleenor, Glen 1953; Foltz, Jae 1942; Foran, Jay 1990; Forbes, Charles 1945; Ford, Gillett 1979-82; Forrest, Chris 1985; Foster, Moses 1974-76; Foussekis, George 1965-67; Fox, Bill 1977; Fox, Rich 1986-89; Francisco, Tommy 1964-66; Frank, Ron 1962-63; Franklin, Milton 1982, 84; Frazee, Barry 1956-57; Frederick, Eustace 1950-51; Freeman, Antonio 1991-94; Freund, Scott 1991; Frontain, Ken 1982-83; Frulla, Bob 1984-86; Fry, Hannon 1980-81; Fry, Keener 1980; Fuerst, Gary 1977; Fuller, Nelson 1941-42, 46; Furrer, Will 1988-91.

G Gaines, Jerry 1971; Gallagher, Jack 1941-42, 46; Galloway, Steve 1972-73, 75; Gambone, John 1978-80; Garber, Barry 1972-74; Garcia, Sal 1964-66; Garland, Roger 1990-91; Gates, Chester 1951; Gaugler, Jim 1936,38; German, Bob 1969-71; Giacolone, Mike 1979-82; Gibson, Keith 1973-76; Gillespie, Dave 1961-62; Gilley, Richard 1948-50; Glatthorn, Bruce 1969-71; Glick, Chris 1994; Good, Rodney 1986-87; Goode, Dick 1961; Goodman, Richard 1948-49; Goodwin, John 1976; Gordon, Leon 1981-84; Gosney, H.W. 1938-39; Gowin, Will 1987-88; Granby, John 1987-89, 91; Grantham, Todd 1985-88; Grantz, Shon 1989; Graves, Preston 1939-40; Gray, Keith 1944; Gray, Torrian 1993-95; Grayson, Shawn 1990, 92; Green, Dave 1961-63; Green, Jerry 1967-69; Green, Larry 1993-95; Green, Newt 1961-63; Greenwood, Todd 1982-85; Gregory, Bob 1962; Griffith, Bob 1965-67; Grinus, Bill 1932; Grizzard, Harold 1951-53; Groom, Tommy 1964-66; Grube, Chad 1989-90; Gwaltney, Dwayne 1984-86.

H Hackbirth, David 1989-90; Hagood, Jay 1993-95; Hair, Tally 1994; Hale, Steve 1985-88; Hall, Bus 1932; Hall, Butch 1968-70; Hall, George 1968-70; Hall, John 1954-56; Hall, Ricky 1979; Hall, Tom 1986-88; Halstead, David 1972-73; Hamilton, J.L. 1945; Hamlin, Jared 1992-94; Hanly, Les 1963-65; Hansrote, Larry 1949-50; Hardee, Billy 1973-75; Haren, Jim 1952-54; Hargrove, Frank 1949-50; Hargrove, James 1989-91; Harman, Rick 1974-75; Harris, Alan 1982, 84-85; Harris, Bob 1958, 60; Harris, Walt 1960; Harrison, Angelo 1995; Hartman, Tom 1982-84; Harvey, Waddey 1966-68; Hawkins, Ron 1961; Hawkins, Scott 1969, 71; Hawkins, Tommy 1962-63; Hayes, Eric 1984-85; Haynes, Jeff 1965-67; Hazzard, Noland 1982-85; Heath, George 1973-76; Hebron, Vaughn 1989-92; Hedrick, Jim 1954, 56; Hegamyer, William 1945, 48; Heizer, Jim 1972-73; Heizer, Mike 1975-77; Henderson, Bert 1967-69; Henderson, Chris 1986-88; Henderson, John 1938-41; Henley, Stacy 1991-94; Henry, Kent 1971-73; Henry, Mel 1935-37; Henry, Pat 1958-59; Herb, Charlie 1950, 52-53; Herdman, Darwin 1987-90; Herndon, John 1954-55, 57; Herndon, Larry 1973; Hess, Bob 1945-47; Hewitt, Wayne 1964; Hickam, Jim 1962-63; Hildebrand, Bill 1969; Hiler, Dick 1950; Hill, Danny 1976-79; Hill, Mike 1981-82; Hill, Robert 1980; Hill, Scott 1986-89; Hilman, J.B. 1951; Hines, Charlie 1959-61; Hite, Billy 1979-82; Hite, Gene 1932; Hobbs, Fran 1950; Hodges, G.D. 1942; Hodges, Mike 1990-92; Hodgson, Andy 1950; Hoestine, G.W. 1933; Hoffman, Joe 1942, 46; Holbrook, Gerald 1960-61; Holbrook, Wynston 1962; Holland, Jeff 1993-95; Holloway, Stephan 1989-91; Holmes, Jermaine 1992, 94-95; Holsclaw, Billy 1956-58; Holsclaw, Duncan 1932-34; Holsclaw, Duncan 1957-58, 60; Holsinger, Ron 1969-71; Holt, Chris 1990-92; Holway, Dickie 1976-78; Hopkins, Archie 1988-90; Hopkins, Orin 1946-49; Horoszko Pete 1971-73; Hosp, Bob 1969; Houff, Tony 1974-76; House Bill 1969-71; Houseright, Bill 1973-77; Houseright, Bill Jr. 1995; Howard, Harry 1934; Howell, Terrence 1982-85; Hromyak, Andy 1971-72; Hudson, Rankin 1938-40; Hudson Robby 1992; Huff, Dick 1949; Huffman, Richard 1932-34; Hughes, Mike 1977-78; Hughes, Tom 1951-53; Hummel, Scott 1990; Humphries, Wayne 1968-69; Hunsucker, Jeff 1971; Hunter, Ben 1959; Hunter, Eddie 1983-86; Hurd, Scott 1975-76; Hvozdovic, Mike 1962-64.

I Ilardo, Leno 1982; Immel, Hank 1968; Inge, Jerry 1973-75; Ingles, Bud 1935-36; Irby, Korey 1994-95; Ittner, Jack 1946-49; Ivanac, John 1969-70.

J Jackson, Pete 1980-81; Jackson, Robby 1983-85; Jackson, Waverly 1993-95; Jacobsen, Steve 1977-81; Jamerson, Bill 1954-55; Jamerson, Phil 1980; James, Bill 1940-42; Jamison,

Randy 1982, 85-86; Jeffries, Jon 1987-88, 91; Jennings, Bryan 1993-95; Johns, Eddie, 1969-71; Johnson, Erick 1964-66; Johnson, James 1977-78; Johnson, Loren 1995; Johnson, Mark 1981, 83-85; Johnson, Mike 1980-83; Johnson, Robert 1946; Johnson, Stacy 1985-86; Johnson, Steve 1984-87; Johnson, Stud 1941-42; Johnson, Ted 1942, 46; Johnson, Vincent 1981-84; Jones, Brad 1989-90; Jones, Calvert 1992; Jones, Dave 1934-36; Jones, Earnie 1984-87; Jones, Grover 1954-56; Jones, Jerry 1983; Jones, Jock 1987-89; Jones, Joe 1980, 82-84; Jones, Lynn 1962-64; Jones, Scott 1990-93; Jones, Victor 1984-87; Joseph, Bernard 1983; Joyce, Eddie 1973; Judy, Ben 1940-42.

K Kapp, Anthony 1995; Karlsen, Bob 1970-72; Kassem, Shakeep 1950; Kautz, J.R. 1945; Keatley, Chip 1976-78; Keeffe, Kevin 1984-87; Keeton, Bunky 1950; Keiffer, Ed 1981-83; Kelly, Dickie 1963-64; Kenley, Mike 1977-78; Kennedy, Tony 1989-92; Kennedy, W.P. 1935; Kerfoot, Billy 1952-54; Kern, Dick 1939-41; Kernan, Charlie 1948-50; Keyes, Howard 1972; Keys, Greg 1981, 83-84; Kidd, Randolph 1987; Kilpatrick, Baird 1988; Kincaid, Al 1967-69; King , Billy 1975-76; King, Brad 1988; King, Chad 1991-92; King, Eric 1978-80; King, E.S. 1937-38; King, Julian 1951-53; Kinzer, Chris 1985-88; Kitts, Jimmy Jr. 1947, 49; Knight, DeWayne 1990-93; Knupp, Kent 1976-78; Koel, Treg 1992-93; Kosco, Joe 1950; Kovac, Mike 1978-80; Kraynak, Ed 1950; Kreiter, Vic 1962-64; Kritsky, Thor 1980-82; Kroehling, J.H. 1946-47; Kuhn, Richard 1949-50; Kujawa, Anthony 1941; Kushner, Larry 1968-70; Kwiatkowski, Frank 1950-52.

L Lagana, Lou 1970; Lambert, Ken 1974; Lamie, David 1975-78; Landrum, Ken 1991-94; Larsen, Atle 1994-95; LaRue, Don 1977-79; Lassiter, Greg 1989-92; Lathan, Kevin 1985-86; Latimer, Wayne 1973-75; Latina, John 1976-78; Laury, Dennis 1979-81; Law, Rick 1974; Lawlar, Tim 1948-50; Lawlor, Bob 1972; Lawrence, Cyrus 1979-82; Lawrence, Paul 1973; Lawson, Bob 1939-41; Lawson, Chip 1973; Lawson, Frank 1942; Lawson, Leland 1957; Ledbetter, Joe 1985, 87; Lee, Ashley 1980-81, 83-84; Leeson, Billy 1982-84; Leland, Harry 1963; Lemmert, Bruce 1972-73; Leonard, Carl 1946-48; Lewis, Ed 1977-78; Lewis, Kenny 1977-79; Lewis, Lawrence 1992-95; Lindon, Ronnie 1966; Lindsey, K.T. 1933; Linson, Billy 1972; Little, Allen 1982-84; Locke, Jim 1954-55; Longerbeam, Dickie 1965, 67-68; LoPresti, Mike 1988; Loria, Frank 1965-67; Lowery, Curt 1973-76; Lucas, Sean 1986, 88-89; Luczak, Ki 1949-51; Ludd, Danny 1973; Ludlow, John 1979-82; Lugar, Jimmy 1956-57; Luongo, Len 1967-68; Luraschi, Ron 1977-81; Luttrell, Bob 1951-54.

M Maccaroni, Warren 1960-61; Maguigan, Ron 1970-72; Maguigan, Steve 1970; Majcher, Stanley 1945; Maksanty, Dick 1971; Malone, Chris 1992-95; Mangum, Bob 1957; Mann, Tim 1984; Marsingill, Luke 1974; Martin, Bobby 1986-89; Martin, Charlie 1972-74; Martin, Kevin 1992-94; Marvel, David 1980-83; Marvin, Tommy 1962-63; Maskas, Marvin 1941-42, 46; Massie, Ray 1960-61; Mast, Howard 1937; Matheny, Chris 1987, 89; Matijevich, Rich 1969-71; Maxwell, John 1967-68; Mays, Eugene 1992; McCall, Brian 1986-89; McCann, Randy 1971-73; McCarter, Keith 1973-76; McClaugherty, C.A. 1941-42; McClung, Marcus 1990-93; McClure, Roger 1940-42; McCoy, Bob 1956; McCoy, Lynn 1973-74; McCraw, Cordell 1947; McDaniel, Bruce 1973-75; McDonald, Carl 1977-80; McDougald, Doug 1976-79; McGinley, Ray 1973; McGinnis, Bill 1960; McGlothlin, Dave 1976; McGuigan, Ron 1964-66; McIntire, J.A. 1932-33; McKee, Tony 1979-82; McMahon, Damien 1991-94; Mead, Matt 1977-79; Meade, Todd 1989-91; Meehan, Kevin 1969-71; Mehr, Tom 1981, 83-85; Mengulas, Gus 1942, 46-47; Meriwether, Otey Jr. 1947-49; Messamore, Claude 1965; Methfessel, Bucky 1977-80; Mickel, Marcus 1988-91; Mihalas, Nick 1956-58; Mikulski, Tim 1968-70; Mikus, Tom 1973; Miles, Shaine 1993-95; Miley, Rick 1979-82; Miller, Al 1937-38; Miller, Andy 1991-94; Miller, Barry 1974-77; Miller, Milt 1966-67; Mills, Ray 1932-33; Minichan, John 1960; Mitchem, Steve 1985-88; Mitchess, Gary 1952; Mollo, Richard 1964, 66-67; Moody, John 1952-53, 56-57; Moon, Russ 1956-57; Moon, Wayne, 1975; Mooney, Dan 1965-67; Morgan, Charlie 1932-33; Morgan, Tim 1989; Moronta, Horacio 1985-86, 88-89; Morrell, Matt 1993-94; Morrison, Tony 1994-95; Moss, Andrew 1990; Moss, Bill 1992; Moss, Joe 1958-59, 61; Moyer, Keith 1994; Mullinax, Greg 1973-75; Mullins, Bubba 1980-81; Murphy, John 1932-33; Murray, R.P. 1935-37; Mutter, Wayne 1978-81; Myers, Billy 1984-87.

N Nash, Joe 1992; Neal, Jay 1974-75; Neal, Lewis 1976-77; Neel, Eddie 1985-87; Neel, Roger 1948-50; Negri, Red 1932-33; Nelson, Clarence 1982-84; Nelson, Jomo 1995; Nelson, Paul 1983-86; Neve, Kyle 1982; Newsome, Myron 1995; Norment, James 1942; Novell, Charles 1977-78; Nutter, Buzz 1950-52; Nuttycombe, Chuck 1975-76.

O O'Brien, Tommy 1958; O'Neale, M.L. 1936; Oakes, Don 1958-60; Ochs, Norman 1933-34; Oliver, Frank 1938; Olson, Hilmer 1956; Onhaizer, Jerry 1977; Onderko, Joe 1951; Orr, Ross 1945-48; Osborne, Danny 1993-94; Otey, Eddie 1980-81; Ottaway, Jim 1934; Owens, Bobby 1964-65; Oxendine, Ken 1994-95.

P Pack, Anthony 1988-91; Page, Darrell 1962-64; Page, Taron 1988; Paige, Tony 1980-83; Paine, Jim 1959-60; Palmer, Benny 1932; Pannell, Jerome 1977-80; Parker, Marcus 1994-95; Parker, Nate 1978-79; Parks, Tom 1968-69; Pasi, Steve 1973; Patterson, Danny 1973; Patterson, James 1982-83; Patterson, Stuart 1974-76; Pavlik, Skip 1988-89; Payne, Greg 1974, 76; Peak, Bob 1961-62; Pearce, Horace Jr. 1942, 46-47; Peduzzi, Chris 1992-94; Peery, Larry 1987-88; Pendleton, Rusty 1989-92; Penn, Jesse 1982-84; Perdue, Chuck 1972-75; Perry, Buddy 1959-61; Perry, Joe 1986; Petrovich, Jim 1992-93; Petty, Doug 1951; Petty, Tom 1951-54; Philbrick, Steve 1973-75; Phillips, Padro 1979-82; Philpot, Larry 1962-63; Pierce, Frank 1936-38; Pigninelli, Jim 1968-70; Piland, O.G. 1934-36; Piland, Rick 1966-68; Pitts, Dave 1938-39; Plank, Stuart 1983, 85; Poindexter, Mark 1990-92; Polascik, John 1983; Polito, Jim 1970-72; Popp, Rick 1973; Porterfield, Bill 1932-33; Powers, Sonny 1938; Prater, Jack 1951, 54-55; Preas, George 1951-54; Preston, Jerome 1989-92; Preston, P.J. 1990-92; Price, J.C. 1992-95; Price, Warren 1960-61; Prioleau, Pierson 1995; Pruett, Art 1959-61; Pryor, John 1983; Pugh, Alger 1957-59; Purdham, Rob 1979-81; Pyne, Jim 1990-93.

Q Quinn, Jimmy 1969-71.

R Raible, John 1964-66; Rand, Erving 1947; Randall, Jim 1952-53, 57; Ransome, Frank 1946; Rapone, Nick 1974, 77-78; Rash, Wayne 1965; Ratcliffe, Barney 1972; Ratliff, Jay 1945, 48-50; Raugh, Ronnie 1950; Razzano, Rick 1974-77; Reaves, Brian 1990-92; Reba, Jim 1966; Reel, Donnie 1971-72; Rehme, John 1989-91; Renner, Bill 1979-82; Reynolds, L.S. 1934-35; Reynolds, Tom 1971-73; Rhodes, Leon 1981-83; Rice, Scott 1986-88, 90; Richards, Jimmy 1965-67; Richards, Tom 1952, 54-55; Richardson, Myron 1986-89; Rider, Scott 1983-85; Ringer, Dick 1958; Ripley, Paul 1967-68; Ritz, John 1981-83; Rivers, John 1990-92; Roane, Morgan 1983-86; Roberts, George 1976-77; Roberts, Jeff 1986-88; Roberts, Steve 1993; Robinette, Roy 1950; Robinson, James 1980-83; Robison, Arthur 1935-37; Robison, Carl 1933; Rodgers, Burt Mack 1962-63; Rogers, Mickey 1977-79; Rogers, Phil 1973-75; Romagnoli, Mike 1977-78; Romero, Tony 1986-87; Rosenbaum, Dick 1950; Roy, Mike 1976; Rucker, John 1941-42; Rudzinski, Don 1974; Runyan, Bruce 1969-71; Russell, Damien 1988-91; Russell, J.D. 1934-35; Russo, Vince 1969-71.

S Sanchez, Eros 1989; Sanders, Steve 1991-93; Sansone, Joe 1977-78; Saunders, Mike 1964-65; Savage, Ellis 1976-78; Scaggs, Steve 1980-82; Scales, Ricky 1972-74; Scales, Shawn 1994-95; Scharnus, Jerry 1971-73; Scharnus, Mike 1978-81; Schmidt, Ben 1956-57; Schmidt, Larry 1975-76; Schneider, John 1970-72; Schnurr, Rodney 1972-73; Schoenadel, Chuck 1972; Schrews, Bill 1974; Schwabe, Gil 1969-70; Schweickert, Bob 1962-64; Scott, Dennis 1976-78; Scott, John 1979-82; Scott, Mark 1990; Scott, Steve 1975-77; Scruggs, Bobby 1952-55; Seal, Bobby 1952; Seaman, Al 1932; Sebeck, Ron 1970; Sedwick, Rod 1971-73; Semones, Brandon 1993-95; Semones, Dennis 1966; Shaffer, Sam 1957-59; Sharpe, J. 1941; Shaw, Mike 1980-83; Shawhan, D.G. 1939; Sheehan, Jerry 1976-78; Sheehy, John 1964-65; Shields, Jon 1993-94; Shipley, John 1964-65; Shirley, Tom 1972-73; Shockey, Carol 1935-37; Shorter, Chuck 1972; Simcsak, Jack 1968-70; Simmons, Roger 1953-55; Simpson, Donnie 1980-81; Singleton, Rick 1985-86; Singleton, Ron 1985-86; Sink, Donald 1954; Sizemore, Aster 1960-62; Skinner, Bill 1968; Slaughter, Bobby 1967-69; Smigelsky, Dave 1978-80; Smith, Alonzo 1982-83; Smith, Bobby 1941, 46-47; Smith, Bruce 1981-84; Smith, Eric 1992; Smith, G.L. 1947; Smith, Gary 1975-78; Smith, Gary 1978-81; Smith, George 1932-34; Smith, Henry 1978; Smith, J.F. 1940; Smith, J.O. 1940; Smith, Jim 1980-82; Smith, Jimmy 1982; Smith, Lamar 1987-90; Smith, Larry 1969-71; Smith, Lenny 1968-70; Smith,

Mike 1992-93; Smith, Okesa 1993, 95; Smith, Pete 1947; Smith, Terry 1990; Smith, Tory 1977-78; Smoot, Terry 1967-69; Snead, Dickie 1957-59; Snell, Donald Wayne 1984-86; Snell, Eddie 1976-77; Snell, Sidney 1977-80; Sodaro, George 1934-36; Soncini, Dale 1972; Spain, Dennis 1990-91; Speck, Charlie 1959-61; Spinner, Baron 1994; Sprenkle, John 1970-72; Sprouse, Donnie 1971-72; Spruill, Hank 1934; Squires, Warren 1949; Stafford, Tommy 1964-66; Staley, E. G. 1945; Stark, William 1950; Steadman, Mark 1976-77; Stephens, Chuck 1958-59; Stevens, Pete 1951; Stevens, Tewon 1992, 94; Stewart, Ramon 1983-84; Stewart, Terry 1971-72; Still, Bryan 1992-95; Stinnette, Wayne 1970-71; Stokes, Don 1986-89; Stollings, Mike 1975-76; Stonesifer, Wayne 1967, 69; Stortz, Bobby 1950; Strager, Duke 1968-70; Streiff, F.A. 1939; Striffler, Pete 1973; Strock, Dave 1970-72; Strock, Don 1970-72; Strock, Tom 1970-72; Stuart, Lewis 1977-80; Stuewe, Michael 1995; Stultz, C.W. 1949; Stump, Bob 1933; Stup, Steve 1984; Sturdivant, Michael 1990-91; Sustek, Mike 1983-84; Swarm, Billy 1991-92; Swarm, Joe 1992-93; Swink, Hunter 1952-53; Swords, Tommy 1968.

T Talbott, Allen 1982-85; Taliaferro, Curtis 1985-86; Taricani, Tom 1984-85; Tate, Ben 1941; Tate, Bill 1939-41; Tate, Steve 1995; Taylor, Alfred 1942; Taylor, Frank 1948-49; Taylor, G.E. 1940; Taylor, Bob 1946-48; Tennessee, Andre 1972-74; Tennis, Ed 1970-71; Testerman, Don 1972; Thacker, Don 1965-67; Thacker, Doug 1973-75; Thomas, Allan 1982-85; Thomas, Bob 1981-84; Thomas, Dave 1932-34; Thomas, Dave 1946-48; Thomas, Dwayne 1992-95; Thomas, Herb 1938-40; Thomas, Jeremiah 1979-82; Thomas, John I. 1995; Thomas, John M. 1995; Thomas, Kent 1982-85; Thomas, Mickey 1989-90; Thomas, Mike 1973; Tiberio, Perry 1968-70; Tilling, Billy 1955, 57; Tilson, Sumner 1945; Toal, Greg 1974; Todd, Andy 1940; Tolley, Rick 1960; Tomblin, Leon 1959-61; Tommelleo, Andy 1979; Trask, Steve 1976-77; Traynham, Pete 1940; Treadwell, Randy 1968; Trice, Tom 1972; Trimble, W.H. 1939; Tucker, Joe 1967-69; Tuggle, John 1982-83; Turner, Joe 1984-86; Turner, Tom 1973-74.

U Udinski, Mark 1979-82; Uglow, Dave 1980; Unger, Phil 1954-55; Unterzuber, R.T. 1940; Urquhart, Cornell 1982-84; Utin, Jon 1965-67; Utz, Kit 1971-72; Utz, Sonny 1962-64.

V Valentine, Craig 1971-72; Vali, Viktor 1988-89; Van Schoick, Craig 1977-80; Varney, Rodney 1986-87; Vaughan, Rob 1987-90; Vaughn, Chad 1995; Vaught, Don 1958-60; Vecellio, Lee 1935-37; Verniel, Marc 1989-92; Vey, Randy 1973-74; Vick, Dwight 1995; Vincent, A.F. 1942; Vishneski, Bernie 1958-60; Vorhies, Bob 1977.

W Wachter, Bob 1949-50; Wade, Don 1981-84; Wade, Tim 1994-95; Waldron, Roe 1977-80; Walker, Leonard 1975-78; Walker, Tommy 1962-63; Wallace, Bill 1973-74; Waller, Quinton 1995; Walton, Harry 1946-48; Warner, P.A. 1941-42; Warriner, George 1938-40; Washington, T.J. 1994-95; Washington, Todd 1995; Watkins, Johnny 1958, 60; Watkins, Paul 1978-79; Watson, Bob 1981-83; Watson, Chuck 1985-87; Watts, Glenn 1987-88, 90; Wauters, Scott 1982; Webb, Mark 1983-86; Webb, Bobby 1946, 48-49; Webb, Tom 1976-79; Webster, Frank 1956; Weihe, Buddy 1961-63; Wellman, B.J. 1945; Welsh, Don 1951-53; Wheatley, Todd 1995; Wheel, Danny 1995; Wheeler, E.H. 1940-41; White, Chad 1950-52; White, Cornelius 1993-95; White, Lawrence 1984-86; White, Ranall 1992-94; White, Richard 1977; Whiteman, Donald 1949; Whitesell, Jay 1957-58; Whitley, Ken 1963-64, 66; Whitten, Jimmy 1987-90; Whittier, Allen 1958-60; Widger, Mike 1967-69; Wiley, Al 1986-87; Wiley, Carter 1984-87; Wilkins, Willie 1993; Williams, Brian 1989, 91; Williams, Jack 1951-53; Williams, Maurice 1983-86; Williams, Michael 1993-94; Williams, Orlando 1984; Williams, Rafael 1992, 95; Williams, Rich 1987-88; Williams, Ryan 1991-94; Willson, Louis 1939; Wilson, Elmer 1941-42, 46; Wilson, Jason 1988-90; Wiltshire, Jack 1991-92; Wimmer, David 1989-92; Windmuller, Denny 1977-78; Winfree, Joe 1973; Wingo, Sterling 1947-50; Wirt, Steve 1977-80; Wolfe, Ernie 1953-54; Wolfenden, Bobby 1954-56; Wood, N.S. 1938; Woody, Sands 1964-66; Woolwine, Jimmy 1940; Wooten, Rodd 1989-91; Worthington, George 1936-38; Wrenn, Pete 1966-67; Wright, Howie 1952-54; Wright, Trevor 1983-84.

Y Yarborough, Frank 1949; Yarborough, William 1992-95; Yeager, George 1981-83; Young, Cam 1988-89; Young, Lawrence 1978-80.

Z Zban, Tom 1991; Zekert, Gerry 1945-47; Zender, Paul 1946; Zeno, Mike 1958-60; Zollicoffer, Ron 1977-78; Zouzalik, Mike 1977-79; Zwinak, B.J. 1980-83; Zydiak, Bill 1939-41;

TRIVIA ANSWERS

1. Branch Bocock.

2. Henry Crisp.

3. The standard-issue practice shoes handed out by equipment manager Lester Karlin.

4. "Mud."

5. Crimson barberry.

6. 1905.

7. No. 9 in 1995 by USA Today/CNN.

8. No. 10 in 1995.

9. Three: Miami (No. 17), Syracuse (No. 20) and Virginia (No. 13).

10. Sun Bowl, 1946.

11. Nine. Sugar (1995), Gator (1994), Independence (1993), Peach (1986), Independence (1984), Peach (1980), Liberty (1968, 1966), Sun (1946).

12. N.C. State defensive back Brian Gay was called for pass interference on Tech wingback David Everett.

13. Terry Strock (Jerry Claiborne and Frank Beamer) and Billy Hite (Bill Dooley and Beamer).

14. Tech 14, Indiana 13.

15. A beat-up steel lunch pail.

16. "Killer."

17. Senior offensive guard Chris Malone (47).

18. Cornell Brown, J.C. Price, George DelRicco, Chris Malone and William Yarborough.

19. Orange tops and orange jerseys — worn in the 1994 Virginia game, a 42-23 loss.

20. Frank Loria, 1967; Bruce Smith, 1984; Jim Pyne, 1993; Cornell Brown, 1995. Pyne was the only unanimous selection.

21. Left guard

22. Williams with 254 points, including 137 from extra points.

23. 1954 (8-0-1).

ABOUT THE AUTHOR

Chris Colston, editor of Virginia Tech's *Hokie Huddler* newspaper for the past 11 years, is now a copy editor for Baseball Weekly, a national publication with a circulation of about 300,000.

Colston — who still contributes a weekly column to the *Huddler* — has personally attended 178 Virginia Tech football games since 1971.

In 1994 and 1995, Colston won "Best In the Nation" awards by the College Sports Information Directors of America for stories that appeared in the Hokie Huddler. Over the last two years CoSIDA named four more of his articles "Best in the District." Tech's district includes such universities as Virginia, North Carolina, Duke, North Carolina State, Wake Forest, South Carolina, Clemson, Miami, Florida State and Florida.

Colston took over the *Huddler* — just

a fledgling in its second year — in June of 1985. Under his direction the paper doubled its circulation.

In his free time Colston wrote general-interest features for the *New River Current*, a supplement of the *Roanoke Times*. Last fall he worked as a college football contributor for the USA Today Information Network. In the summer of 1995 he authored the athletic department's brochure as part of a multi-million dollar university-wide fund-raising campaign.

Colston, 38, resides in Alexandria, Va.

COLLEGE SPORTS HANDBOOKS

Stories, Stats & Stuff About America's Favorite Teams

U. of Arizona	Basketball	Arizona Wildcats Handbook
U. of Arkansas	Basketball	Razorbacks Handbook
Baylor	Football	Bears Handbook
Clemson	Football	Clemson Handbook
U. of Colorado	Football	Buffaloes Handbook
U. of Florida	Football	Gator Tales
Georgia Tech	Basketball	Yellow Jackets Handbook
Indiana U.	Basketball	Hoosier Handbook
Iowa State	Sports	Cyclones Handbook
U. of Kansas	Basketball	Crimson & Blue Handbook
Kansas State	Sports	Kansas St Wildcat Handbook
LSU	Football	Fighting Tigers Handbook
U. of Louisville	Basketball	Cardinals Handbook
U. of Miami	Football	Hurricane Handbook
U. of Michigan	Football	Wolverines Handbook
U. of Missouri	Basketball	Tiger Handbook
U. of Nebraska	Football	Husker Handbook
U. of N. Carolina	Basketball	Tar Heels Handbook
N.C. State	Basketball	Wolfpack Handbook
U. of Oklahoma	Football	Sooners Handbook
Penn State	Football	Nittany Lions Handbook
U. of S. Carolina	Football	Gamecocks Handbook
Stanford	Football	Stanford Handbook
Syracuse	Sports	Orange Handbook
U. of Tennessee	Football	Volunteers Handbook
U. of Texas	Football	Longhorns Handbook
Texas A&M	Football	Aggies Handbook
Texas Tech	Sports	Red Raiders Handbook
Wichita State	Sports	Shockers Handbook
U. of Wisconsin	Football	Badgers Handbook

Also:

Big 12 Handbook: Stories, Stats and Stuff About The Nation's Best Football Conference

The Top Fuel Handbook: Stories, Stats and Stuff About Drag Racing's Most Powerful Class

For ordering information call Midwest Sports Publications at:

1-800-492-4043